CAMBRIDGE TEXTS AND STUDIES IN THE HISTORY OF EDUCATION

General Editors

A. C. F. BEALES, A. V. JUDGES, J. P. C. ROACH

THOMAS ARNOLD ON EDUCATION

IN THIS SERIES

Texts

Fénelon on Education, edited by H. C. Barnard

Friedrich Froebel, a selection edited by Irene Lilley

Matthew Arnold and the Education of the New Order,
edited by Peter Smith and Geoffrey Summerfield

Robert Owen on Education, edited by Harold Silver

James Mill on Education, edited by W. H. Burston

Samuel Hartlib and the Advancement of Learning,
edited by Charles Webster

Thomas Arnold on Education, edited by T. W. Bamford

Studies

Education and the French Revolution, by H. C. Barnard

OTHER VOLUMES IN PREPARATION

THOMAS ARNOLD ON EDUCATION

A SELECTION FROM HIS WRITINGS
WITH INTRODUCTORY
MATERIAL BY

T. W. BAMFORD

Deputy Director
University of Hull Institute of Education

CAMBRIDGE
AT THE UNIVERSITY PRESS
1970

CAMBRIDGE UNIVERSITY PRESS
Cambridge, New York, Melbourne, Madrid, Cape Town, Singapore,
São Paulo, Delhi

Cambridge University Press
The Edinburgh Building, Cambridge CB2 8RU, UK

Published in the United States of America by
Cambridge University Press, New York

www.cambridge.org
Information on this title: www.cambridge.org/9780521110266

First published 1970
This digitally printed version 2009

A catalogue record for this publication is available from the British Library

Library of Congress Catalogue Card Number: 79–108099

ISBN 978-0-521-07785-9 hardback
ISBN 978-0-521-11026-6 paperback

CONTENTS

Acknowledgements   *page* vii

Abbreviations   viii

Introduction   1

  Life and Problems   1

  Religious Ideas and Education   5

  Social Ideas and Education   12

  Other Educational Views   19

  Sources and Influences   29

  Arnold's Method of Writing   37

  Note on the Selections   41

WRITINGS ON EDUCATION

Education and the Social Classes   45

Christian Education   68

The Problems of Boyhood   78

The Role, Character and Duties of a
  Headmaster and Staff   94

The Art of Teaching   102

Education in School   106

The Future Occupations of Boys   144

The Universities   151

Notes   167

Chronological Table   169

Select Bibliography   175

Index   177

[v]

ACKNOWLEDGEMENTS

I would like to thank Professor Judges and the editors for the opportunity of contributing to the series, *Cambridge Texts and Studies in the History of Education*.

The material from books has been gathered from the libraries of the British Museum, the University of Hull, and the University of Hull Institute of Education. Original Arnold letters have been seen in the British Museum, British Transport Commission Archives, the Brotherton Library, University of Leeds, while photostat copies have been obtained from the County Archives, Shire Hall, Warwick, and from the collection of Mr Cahalin.

It is a pleasure to acknowledge the help given by many people, including Mr Cahalin of Sutton Coldfield for bibliographical advice and information: Mr Freeman and Mr Hooton of the University of Hull for help in tracing appropriate editions; Mr Honey of the University of Durham for discussion on public-school problems.

ABBREVIATIONS

MW   *The Miscellaneous Works of Thomas Arnold.*

QJEd   *Quarterly Journal of Education.*

SL   Letter in *Stanley's Life of Thomas Arnold D.D.*
Teachers' Edition 1901. The initials (SL) are
followed by the number of the letter, date and
the relevant page. It should be noted that the
numbering of the letters differs from that in the
first edition of 1844. Thus letter no. LXV in
volume 1 of the 1844 edition becomes LXXVI in
1901. Similarly letter no. XCVIII of volume 2 of
the 1844 edition becomes no. CXIII in 1901. The
1901 edition, in spite of its faults, has been
chosen for reference purposes here because it is
easily the most readily available of all editions.
A further complication arises in the version
edited by G. T. Bettany (undated) for the
Minerva Library of Famous Books, based on
the sixth edition, and given the original title:
*The Life and Correspondence of Thomas Arnold
D.D.* by Arthur Penrhyn Stanley. Five letters
additional to those of the 1901 edition appear in
this volume. The reader will find it easier, unless
the 1901 edition is to hand, to trace letters by
using the date of the letter concerned rather
than the other information.

Sermons The volume number of the sermons refers to
the 1878 collected edition. See the bibliography
for the relationship of the 1878 volumes to the
original (unnumbered) editions.

INTRODUCTION

LIFE AND PROBLEMS

Thomas Arnold was born in 1795 at Cowes in the Isle of
Wight, the youngest of a large family of seven children. It
was an ambitious professional household, a little uncertain
of its place in society and anxious to resolve and consoli-
date its position by good marriage and education. Accordingly young Thomas was put through the fairly typical
schooling of a person in his position and learnt the rudiments from his father and his aunt before going to school
at Warminster in Wiltshire. He was an eccentric rebellious
boy, difficult to handle, and after a few years he went on to
Winchester and finally to the university. At Oxford he
entered into his happiest and most fruitful period to which
he looked back nostalgically all his life. He was entranced
with the town, found the conditions ideal for study and
obtained a first in 1815. What was more important, he also
formed useful friendships that helped him at all stages of
his life, into his first post at Oriel and even to the headmaster's chair at Rugby. At twenty-four he fell in love,
and in view of the rather limited university prospects he
became a schoolmaster, taking in private pupils alongside
his brother-in-law in the Thames-side village of Laleham.
There he spent the next nine years with his rapidly growing
family, leading a quiet life interspersed with holidays
abroad and writing articles. As time passed he became more
and more restless and at last was urged by his friends to
apply for the post at Rugby. There, his life suddenly took
on a new confidence, urgency and success; his period of
influence and controversy had begun.

The bare bones of such a career do not reveal anything
unusual or dramatic, and normally it would have anticipated a relatively uneventful if successful life, similar to

hundreds of others in the nineteenth century. In spite of
that Arnold became a seminal figure in the church, a
champion of the new order; he became too an anonymous
political thinker and acquired the reputation of a reformer
of public schools, the feature for which he is best known
today. What made Arnold different from the rest? Was it
just a question of ability or were background and character
important?

As a youth he was rebellious, and, although there were
instances of physical resistance, it was mainly a rebellion
of the mind. The setting of England at that period encouraged such an attitude, and there were plenty of kindred
spirits in a society that was shaken by the American and
French revolutions, followed by the long Napoleonic
conflict. Moreover, the rapidly developing industrial
scene saw the rise of social unrest, suppressed during the
war, but flaring into riots after Waterloo.

Arnold was undoubtedly affected by these matters, the
war in his early years and the social problems later in life,
when the agitation and the threat of revolt perturbed him
greatly: 'But I feel the state of public affairs so deeply,
that I cannot bear either to read, or hear, or speak, or write
about them.'[1]

At the same time he was a classicist by upbringing and
an historian at heart. He was certainly more concerned
with Hannibal and Caesar than with Wellington and
Napoleon. Even so, the rebellious streak, so marked in his
youth, persisted and became the dominant feature of his
manhood. With most people the spirit of rebellion grows
thinner as studies inevitably grow deeper and become
more complex, and especially as they acquire the responsibilities of life and marriage, but for Arnold the opposite
was the case. The more complex the material became the
better he relished it and the more he was able, to his satis-

---

[1] *SL*, cciii, 23 August 1839, p. 513.

faction at least, to include the new elements into his reform programme, until ultimately he had created a grand overall pattern based on a simple skeletal framework. As a result he adjusted everything to his own vision, rather than the reverse, and he became interested in reform both as a concept in itself and as a process across the whole span of human endeavour. Although he yearned to enter the reform battle personally and did in fact try to influence matters by writing and creating a newspaper, Arnold remained essentially a theoretician and an onlooker, as may be seen in the social and church fields. In social terms he lived in stirring times with erupting incidents in Peterloo and the riots; but in fact his own life was far removed from the troubles and, apart from a very short period, he lived all his days in country towns and villages well away from the slums, the smells and the social unrest. His interests here as elsewhere were really concerned with his own theoretical designs for the world and the necessity for seeing that the right decisions were made to give them meaning. In church affairs and in his continued attack on the Oxford Movement he played a vital role, but again in terms of writing only—the real battles were left to his disciples and those who thought like him. If he had been a bishop, no doubt he would have carried the fight directly to the enemy; but his Rugby duties prevented that. The fact is that to Arnold reform was the driving force of his thinking in social affairs, politics and religion, and that this was related to an ideal model for society he had created in the grand manner of Plato and Aristotle. Only towards the very end of his life, in his middle forties, are there signs that his ardour was beginning to fade and that he was looking forward to an easier life, in spite of his grandiose plans to force the pace of reform by a national survey.

Some of these matters—his social, religious, and educational ideas together with his influence and writings—are developed in the following sections. The effort to gather together all these ideas from such disparate fields into one framework did not really produce simplicity in the man himself. He was indeed an extremely complex person whose actual life and theoretical concepts were often in different worlds. This has led to the charge of hypocrisy by his critics and certainly, on any superficial analysis, his life presents us with a network of paradoxes which must be faced if we are to understand his character and ways of thought.

Thus he was deeply religious, preaching humility; yet he was also very worldly, and in spite of his condemnation of vanity, anxious to be recognised and rewarded by the world and those in authority for his true worth. He drew his religious, moral and mental inspiration almost entirely from the remote past, and physically retraced the paths of history in Italy and elsewhere, and yet he was even more vitally concerned with the applications of history and the evolution of present day society. Again, he emphasised continually the significance of law and order but rejoiced in revolution. Similarly he took great pride in the concept of the stability provided by the English landed gentry and aristocracy and yet he championed lower-class rights, looking forward to a phased lower-class revolution and lower-class control. His way of life as represented by his households, cultural ways and travel was essentially that of the gentry and yet he castigated that way of life, in its normal meaning and implications, as sinful. In this connection, although he wished to apply reform to all institutions, he exempted his own family from its consequences, since he wanted to strengthen its roots in the past, gentry fashion, and create a sense of continuity.

On the educational side, he had a very large family but

he did not really understand children at all; he ran a public school but his heart was in the religious and social struggles outside the gates. Again, he adored the classics and despised the moderns, but thought the future hope of mankind lay with industry. As a headmaster it was his duty to educate and prepare boys for the professions and yet openly he despised these occupations. Even after he died the paradox remains, for he is said to have reformed the public schools whereas in fact there is precious little evidence of it.

RELIGIOUS IDEAS AND EDUCATION

The one unshakeable basis of Arnold's religion was a belief in the divinity of Christ. Everything else was human, almost trivial, and in continual need of critical and rational assessment. The church itself was a useful and necessary institution, but nothing more. It was man-made and as such should be attacked with the same vigour as politicians or parliament. For Arnold criticism was not adverse comment but a sign of concern and love—the more you loved an institution the more you should seek to reform it. At the same time reform must be legitimate; it must only come from within the institution, from those members who were genuinely interested in its preservation. Anyone who wished to change the basic nature and freedom of the institution, thereby destroying its independence, he regarded as treacherous. This principle lay at the root of his bitterness against Newman and the Tractarians:

My feelings towards a Roman Catholic are quite different from my feelings towards a Newmanite, because I think the one a fair enemy, the other a treacherous one. The one is a Frenchman in his own uniform...the other is the Frenchman disguised in a red coat, and holding a post within our praesidia, for the purpose of betraying it. I should honour the first, and hang the second.[1]

Arnold could not agree on the significance of the apostolic succession, its historical and divine background, the exclusiveness of the powers of priests (priestcraft), the divorce of the church from lay influence, the condemnation of parliamentary links and the isolation of the church from the social problems of the times. Similarly he was against chanting, excessive ceremonial, incense and the like. The common ground between him and the Tractarians lay simply in the divinity of Christ and little else.

In contrast to the spirit of Newmanism, Arnold wanted the church to adopt an active, positive role in the concepts of state and citizenship, christianity should be the moral binding force comparable to the political element of parliament. To this end a fusion of churches was necessary to incorporate the people within one community, and he insisted that this was not just a dream, but a practical policy since all christians had the same fundamental bond. It was in the first instance particularly feasible for the anglican and dissenting churches, and he spelt out the details in his *Principles of Church Reform* (1833): 'wherever there are...ministers of different denominations, the Church [of the parish] might be kept open ready the whole of the Sunday...the different services being fixed at different hours, and performed by different ministers'.[2] True statehood was the aim, and the citizen of such a state owed allegiance not only to the law and the fundamental institutions of state, but also to the moral law, which, in

[1] *SL*, CCLXXXIV, 30 October 1841, p. 617. Such vehemence was common in his letters, which for some might be regarded as privileged and private, but such thoughts are also found in publications as well, e.g. see 'The Oxford Malignants and Dr Hampden', *Edinburgh Review* (April 1836).

[2] *Principles of Church Reform*, 1833, p. 68.

the case of England, meant christianity.[1] Thus Jews, Moslems and non-christians, including Unitarians, could not partake of English citizenship.

The adaptation of these principles to education led Arnold into difficulties. Education was moral and, apart from the subtle inculcations of belief in childhood, could only start after the rudiments were established and the person could begin to appreciate the problems involved. Also, in view of the childhood associations and allegiances, the moral framework could only be built around the particular behaviour of the family concerned. Since the majority of the people in England were christian the moral fibre of the nation must be christian also; it followed that the education of the English citizen must follow suit. This need for a national christian system of education led to his stand against the efforts to make London University non-religious and secular—a resistance he carried to the point of resignation.[2] The problem of the different sects was, of course, a real one, but Arnold's solution was not to eliminate the essential religious nature of education or to compromise on impossibles but to provide alternative arrangements. Non-christians could not have citizenship, but they had a right to education. Jews, Unitarians and others must receive moral instruction acceptable to their beliefs, and at the universities new halls should be specially set up for them. It followed from this that in another non-christian country a different basis for education and citizenship should exist—in Egypt, for instance, the education must be based on Islam.

In school Arnold gave the christian–anglican spirit priority over all other studies and insisted that all pupils pay adequate attention to it. He would not, for instance,

[1] For relevant extracts and the social context of this, see pp. 156–9 etc.
[2] See pp. 163–4.

knowingly admit Unitarians to the school. At the same time this attitude was a personal one and not necessarily binding on his staff; indeed in one celebrated instance, involving correspondence, he was willing for the boy to remain in the charge of another member of the staff at Rugby but not in the Sixth, which was his own responsibility.[1] This apparent tolerance on a subject in which he felt so deeply is impressive and yet it makes his intransigence over London University and over other questions difficult to understand. Perhaps the answer lies in his concept of the ideal professionalism of teachers in which each member of staff has a right to his own opinions and actions on the pattern of the Oxford or Cambridge don. At the same time it should not be assumed that tolerance was an essential part of Arnold's nature. It was not; he was quite intolerant over evil; and over sociological problems he could be utterly ruthless, even brutal and callous over long continuous periods, as shown by his actions at Rugby in the treatment of very young boys in his care.

Arnold's belief in Christ and the eternal meant that the world was merely a testing ground and a preparation for the life hereafter. He felt that not only was he in charge of boys but he was responsible for their souls and ultimate fate. Entry to the next world was only possible by the good life, by the conscious building of a sufficient stock of virtue and an equal effort at repelling evil. Evil was something positive that Arnold could almost see and feel. When faced with it he would rise in anger and could, indeed, on occasions completely lose his self-control; while on more formal occasions in chapel, when considering it in the abstract, he would rave and cry in the pulpit. It is impossible to read the sermons in their entirety without receiving the vision of a man in torment.[2]

[1] See p. 76.　　[2] For the nature of his sermons see p. 167 n. 1.

Evil was a key concept. He saw it as partly inherited and partly acquired. Innocence to him was a sham and tantamount to a denial of original sin. A person's misdeeds and misthoughts were balanced against virtue and the net profit or loss totted up like money in a cash register, with the culprit answerable for the total in the final reckoning. This applied not only to adults and boys as individuals, but to their masters also, who would be responsible if they avoidably allowed the boy's soul to slip. Six evils were evident at school—profligacy, falsehood, bullying, disobedience, idleness and the magnetism of evil.[1] At other times he offered also extravagance and childishness. He followed the consequences of some of these into the pastimes of youth. The growing habit of reading popular books and serials of the Pickwick variety had become an obsession and was absorbing the time and attention of boys to an extent that they could not really afford. And, by finding satisfaction and excitement in these stories, they no longer found any satisfaction in their studies.[2]

From the catalogue of evil there is one startling omission. No mention is made of sex anywhere. Although he was continually talking and writing about evil and the problems of evil, itemising the various types and elaborating on their nature, nonetheless we have to read between the lines and guess at the sexual innuendoes when he is actually considering gluttony or sensuality or drunkenness. The nearest approach comes in one of the sermons: 'The actual evil which may exist in a school consists, I suppose, first of all in direct sensual wickedness, such as drunkenness and other things forbidden together with drunkenness in the Scriptures.'[3]

Both he and the boys knew that the problem of homosexuality was the most serious one of all, but the code of

---

[1] See pp. 86–91.   [2] See pp. 141–3.
[3] *Sermons*, vol. 5, p. 66. See pp. 86–91 for fuller extract.

the times prevented it from being mentioned. This continual skirting round the point, without ever reaching it, seems a little comic to us now, especially as most of the boys came from backgrounds without the usual Victorian inhibitions to sex. In one sense Arnold and the staff were the centre of a sandwich—with the boys knowing far more about sex than they would admit, and the Trustees, coming mostly from the gentry and aristocracy, viewing the staff with amused tolerance for their primness.[1]

But evil, whether of the open type or the unmentionable, grew rapidly among new boys soon after entry; it was triggered off by the new social setting and generally prospered when boys were gathered together; conversely it declined with solitude. This period of moral lapse Arnold equated with boyhood, and he saw the sequence of childhood, boyhood and manhood as a kind of instinctive unfolding of the past, thereby reflecting the changes which had taken place in man's ancestral history in a manner reminiscent of Darwin and Jung.[2] By and large there was a correlation between the total evil recorded for one person and the quantity of original sin. Original sin was inherited in an amount dependent on one's parents and similarly transmitted in large or small amounts to one's children. Those with large amounts of original sin (recognised by their deeds and convictions) had little chance of redemption; they must be shunned and so must their children. This is a hard doctrine, but, admitting the postulate of original sin, it is logical. Expulsion was not a punishment so much as a means of ridding the school of

---

[1] One problem was the clergyman role of the masters. It might have had social status importance and moral implications for the *loco parentis* situation, but it also cut them off from everyone in the community as carriers of false standards and moral levels. The uneasy atmosphere in mixed civilian-clergyman groups is still noticeable today and was most marked in the last century.

[2] See p. 91.

polluting influences; it was therefore an absolute necessity. Expulsion was also needed for those older boys who had failed in their studies and, lacking intellectual stimulation, might succumb to the alternative attractions of evil. Flogging also had its place in this society since the boy must choose between bodily discomfort and mental and private glee.

Innocence was something Arnold did not understand. It contradicted the concept of original sin and therefore the 'innocent' face in boyhood and beyond was suspect. On these occasions when Arnold felt himself face to face with the devil his fury was frightening and his flogging severe. Within every boy there was or ought to be a struggle, and the fight between good and evil must be manifest in the developing youth. Furthermore, not only should the youth be visibly conquering evil, but the true christian spirit was to be demonstrated in practical ways by an interest in and personal knowledge of poverty, sickness and old age. What was really wanted was a manly approach—manly, christian thoughtfulness or a manly and christian standard of duty:

Common idleness and absolute ignorance are not what I wish to speak of now, but a character advanced above these; a character which does not neglect its school-lessons, but really attains to considerable proficiency in them; a character at once regular and amiable, abstaining from evil, and for evil in its low and grosser forms, having a real abhorence. What, then, you will say, is wanting here? I will tell you what seems to be wanting,—a spirit of manly, and much more of Christian, thoughtfulness. There is quickness and cleverness; much pleasure, perhaps, in distinction, but little in improvement; there is no desire of knowledge for its own sake, whether human or divine. There is, therefore, but little power of combining and digesting what is read; and, consequently, what is read passes away, and takes no root in the mind. This same character shows itself in matters of conduct; it will adopt, without scruple, the most foolish, common-place notions of boys, about what is right and wrong;

it will not, and cannot, from the lightness of its mind, concern itself seriously about what is evil in the conduct of others, because it takes no regular care of its own, with reference to pleasing God; it will not do anything low or wicked, but it will sometimes laugh at those who do; and it will by no means take pains to encourage, nay, it will sometimes thwart and oppose anything that breathes a higher spirit, and asserts a more manly and Christian standard of duty.[1]

This approach requires a very mature individual and it is not surprising that very few boys lived up to the Doctor's expectations.

SOCIAL IDEAS AND EDUCATION

Arnold was a student of demographic trends, and the social and economic problems arising from changes in population. He agreed with Malthus that the crux of the situation was: '*the tendency of population to outgrow the means of subsistence.* So that, to use Aristotle's words, a limitation of property is nothing, unless you can also limit within proper bounds the increase of population...the Malthusian theory of population...was known to Aristotle and to the philosophers of ancient Greece, quite as well as to Mr. Malthus.'[2]

According to Arnold there were two periods of population crisis in a nation's growth, the first corresponding to the introduction of more efficient industry (as in England in the middle of the sixteenth century), the second coinciding with the systematic improvement of physical resources and national wealth combined with national poverty:

To this second period we are come, and to the time when its crisis is most threatening. The great point on which I would insist is this;—that let railways be multiplied as they will, or new markets opened for our manufactures, or still further

---

[1] *Sermons*, vol. 4, pp. 37-8.   [2] *MW*, p. 191.

improvements introduced into agriculture, still our population will continue to be excessive so long as the wages of labour are low, and the bulk of the people depend solely on their labour. And this will continue to be the case, until the habits and tastes of the poor can be raised, and they can be taught to look for better prospects for their children than merely keeping them from starving. I come to the conclusion, therefore, that our population requires to be lessened.[1]

This linkage of excess population, poverty and such devices as emigration, colonies and service overseas, obsessed Arnold throughout life, from the time of his first work, delivered at Oxford on 7 June 1815, six days before his twentieth birthday.[2]

One marked contrast between ancient and Victorian civilisations was the existence of slavery, and this led naturally to a comparison between slaves and the poor, with the associated aspects of property and freedom:

Freedom and property are things so essentially united that to have a large free population *wholly* dependent on their labour, when that labour is of a sort which every man can perform, is of itself a state of things fraught with mischief. Perhaps some of your readers [*Sheffield Courant*] may not be aware that this state is one of rare occurrence in the history of the world; because, generally speaking, either the great mass of labourers have been slaves, or else their numbers have been much below the resources of the country, and their market has been so good that industry has enabled them to acquire property. Now when the labourers were slaves, their welfare as little entered into the consideration of statesmen as that of the brute creation; the happiness of the *nation* was never thought to be affected because its *slaves* were oppressed and miserable. In truth this was the readiest way of solving the problem, how to ensure the happiness of civil society—shut out from society those whom it is most difficult to render happy[3]... our poor at this moment have the name and rights of freemen, while their outward condition is that of

[1] *MW*, p. 194.
[2] 'The Effects of Distant Colonization on the Parent State.'
[3] Reflections of this are to be seen in the works of Whitehead and Peter Drucker.

slaves. And this is the case, because we have transferred to our free population the notions which were entertained of a population of slaves: because labourers, when slaves, had and could have, no property, we have thought it no evil that labourers when citizens should be equally destitute.[1]

Emigration as a policy to alleviate the problem could only be practicable with willing cooperation, and this could only be achieved by educating the emigrant.[2] Arnold drew interesting parallels between this lower-class emigration and the upper and upper-middle-class tendency to send excess sons to India and the empire,[3] a feature which we look on nowadays as one of the major roles of public schools in Victorian times.

The lack of financial backing for the poor reduced them to the level of cattle, and the ethos of their way of life prevented them from self-advancement. At the same time, Arnold was fond of complaining that relationships were not helped by employers who talked of 'hands' and ignored the people attached to them. It was a denial of essential dignity:

A man sets up a factory, and *wants hands*...the loan of their *hands*;—of their heads and hearts he thinks nothing. These *hands* are attached to certain mouths and bodies which must be fed and lodged, but this must be done as cheaply as possible;— and accordingly, up starts a miserable row of houses, built where ground is cheapest...as close as possible, to have the more of them to a given space, and for the same reason without any sort of garden or outlet attached to them, because the comfort and enjoyment of the human being is quite independent of the serviceableness of his *hands*. But...these *hands* are not only attached to mouths and bodies, but to reasonable minds and immortal souls.[4]

As such the lower classes were a danger and a menace, so that anything which promised in the end to raise their

[1] *MW*, pp. 196–7.   [2] See p. 148.
[3] See pp. 147–8.   [4] *MW*, pp. 209–10. See also *ibid.* p. 456.

standards met with his approval. Hence his admiration and championship of the potential of railways, factories, the industrial revolution, radical reform, the revolutions in France, and also his effort to bring about understanding between the upper and lower classes.

The nature of citizenship was an essential element in the theoretical conception of any future state, and here Arnold found his classical and historical vision particularly significant:

That bond and test of citizenship then which the ancient legislatures were compelled to seek in sameness of race, because thus only could they avoid the worst of evils, a confusion and consequent indifference in men's notions of right and wrong, is now furnished to us in the profession of Christianity. He who is a Christian, let his race be what it will, let his national customs be ever so different from ours, is fitted to become our fellow citizen: for his being a Christian implies that he retains such of his national customs only as are morally indifferent; and for all such we ought to feel the most perfect toleration. He who is not a Christian, though his family may have lived for generations on the same soil with us, though they may have bought and sold with us, though they may have been protected by our laws, and paid taxes in return for that protection, is yet essentially not a citizen but a sojourner; and to admit such a person to the rights of citizenship tends in principle to the confusion of right and wrong, and lowers the objects of political society to such as are merely physical and external.[1]

Christianity was both a bonding agent and a detector. Without it a person had no right to full citizenship in a christian country and this principle, as we have seen, had some immediate consequences on education, particularly for the admission to the universities of Jews, Unitarians and others.

Fundamental to his ideas on both social duty and education was the idea of responsibility and the maintenance of stability. Here property was essential: 'It is considered in

[1] *MW*, pp. 395–6.

our days that those who are possessed of property in a
country ought to be citizens in it: the ancient maxim was,
that those who were citizens ought to be possessed of
property.'[1]

Property and responsibility lay at the base of his hope
for the education of the lower classes. They left school too
early to be educated and were too busy thereafter to
acquire it later. Moreover the life of the poorer classes
made the very idea of education ludicrous—social improvement must come first. The situation was urgent, arising
from the dilemma that political power must inevitably
pass to the masses; and yet the exercise of that power
needed education which the social condition denied. The
only way out of this impasse was education derived by
other means and the hope that this education would create
demands for the better education of their children. One
vehicle for this was responsibility—the lower classes must
be made to look after their own cultural and welfare
services. Another was to reverse the attitude of the lower
classes to property, since the possession of property
produced an attitude of mind which combined reflection,
caution and forethought. However simple this was in
theory, there were formidable difficulties: 'Having no
property of their own they hate property—having no
means of intellectual enjoyment, they are driven to seek
the pleasures which we have in common with brutes.'[2]

Property and education were interlinked but there was
also a Malthus effect:

It is more than two thousand years ago that a Greek philosopher,
Phaleas of Chalcedon, impatient, like Mr. Owen in the present
day, of the existing evils of society, proposed to remedy them
by an equalization of property and of education. Upon the first
of these remedies Aristotle remarks, that a limit set to property
is inefficient, unless you also set a limit to population. Otherwise,

[1] *MW*, p. 396, note a.   [2] *MW*, p. 211.

says he, your system in the first place cannot last, and besides you will in the course of a few years have as much poverty as ever.[1]

Arnold saw the future of England as a country composed of christian property owning educated citizens. Christianity would supply the institutional framework and a moral basis, but the mass of the nation was, as yet, uneducated and therefore irresponsible. In the short run the country stood in need of a leadership which could only come from the church and the aristocracy: 'I say plainly,—and I beg not to be cried down unheard,—that those great means of blessing are the *Aristocracy* and the *Christian Church*.'[2] But the aristocracy (including the gentry) were, with few exceptions, unfitted for the task at present—they had potential only and needed a drastic shock to bring about a conversion to their true role:

Let the Reform Bill now pass...and the higher classes will have a spur to virtuous exertion which may be a double blessing to themselves and to the country. Influence must henceforth be deserved, not commanded: but desert can yet win it—and the world never yet saw a race of men better fitted to win it than the nobility and gentry of England, if once roused from the carelessness of an undisputed ascendency.[3]

The situation was on a knife edge, and in moments of doubt Arnold feared that the aristocracy would never make it. Indeed, some of his most fierce condemnations were for the aristocrats who lived luxuriously, divorced from life on their estates, out of touch with the masses they ought to lead.[4] For this to be possible the classes must draw together in sympathy.

The perfection of Parliamentary Reform would be one which so raised the working classes, as to oblige the aristocracy to treat

[1] *MW*, p. 191.
[2] *MW*, p. 213. In modern terminology we would talk of elites.
[3] *The Englishman's Register*, No. 2, 14 May 1831.
[4] See *SL*, ccxxxv, 12 April 1840, for a typical outburst.

them more liberally, without throwing in their hands an exorbitant power before they are instructed, and softened enough to use it wisely. I wish the aristocracy in every place to come forward manfully, to join the political unions, or any other lawful and honest societies of the working classes, to state fairly the amount of their past neglect, and their hearty wish to make up for it.[1]

In other words the leadership of the aristocracy was urgently needed now, in the transition period, before the inevitable change in the balance of power. These views were held at times of unrest and doubt, as in the Reform Bill period and Chartist troubles. At times in between, when the dangers appeared to subside, his faith in the aristocracy returned and he considered them as a key element in the stability of England.[2] It must be stressed that all these hopes and fears were linked with the necessity for lower class reform, for he was generally in favour of the 'People's Charter' and had a vision of the future of the lower class that was far rosier than many of the Chartists themselves.

One obvious result of this line of thought, as applied to education, was the inculcation of the spirit of leadership in his own boys at Rugby so that they would perform their rightful function in adult life.

Arnold was, after all, the headmaster of a school for the sons of the upper-class landed gentry and rich professionals. The ideal was for the school to run itself—a boy society with the staff on the sidelines. It was a kind of democracy with many people achieving power in turn, and learning the business of life and obedience through fagging. Within this organisation, leadership, obedience and duty would all be manifest at different levels. But

---

[1] *MW*, p. 214.
[2] For this variable attitude, see *SL*, CLXVI, 6 December 1837; *SL*, XCV, 4 March 1835; *SL*, CLXXX, 18 May 1838; *SL*, CCXVIII, 23 January 1840.

Arnold's concept of leadership was not the mythological figure of a public school product running the country or administering vast areas of India by a kind of divine right. Leadership was a transitional caretaker phase until it was possible to bring about a shared responsibility throughout the entire country, however far off that might be. Indeed the moral and character problems of leadership were so great that he almost appears at times to reject the concept as undesirable, as in his statements on the armed forces, the professions of law and medicine and the empire.[1]

OTHER EDUCATIONAL VIEWS

Some of Arnold's basic views on education are interlocked with those on the church, the state and the social system, and as such have been considered in those contexts. These refer particularly to the religious and christian content of education including the nature of evil, the significance of character and expulsions, the moral issues, the concept of citizenship and the preparation for it. There are, however, other educational matters of significance.

Arnold had doubts about public schools and he expressed them on many occasions; he was not convinced that they provided the best education in the sense that a parent, faced with the schooling of his own son and having no financial worries to deter him ought to settle automatically for a public school.[2] The education was good when the school was good, but the quality could change so rapidly with a new master or a new circle of boys that choosing was hazardous in the extreme. We see this dilemma develop as a personal affair when he sent two sons to

[1] For some of his views on these occupations, see pp. 144–6, 149–50.
[2] See p. 53.

Winchester. The doubts stemmed mainly from the boarding element. The family and the parental home was the best place for growing boys, and he stressed repeatedly the advantages of being a day scholar at a public school. In this way the boy would get the benefit of the school without the vice associated with boarding. To some extent this was connected with the problem of so-called innocence in childhood under parents, and the desirability of continuing to insulate the child from the evil to which he would otherwise be exposed at school in the moral weaning period.

Against this the famous public schools offered certain advantages. The boys formed lasting friendships with people of substance, and these would be useful throughout life. Equally the aura of antiquity in the old schools gave a kind of mystical fusion of the present with past generations, producing a vision of the centuries, and of the school immersed in past problems of the nation and contributing to their solution. For this long-term involvement, size was important since it ensured stability and security.[1] At Rugby the buildings had just been erected by Wooll; they were magnificent but new, and this newness worried Arnold who tried to increase their significance by the addition of stained glass.

It is usually considered that the headmaster of a public school should understand and be in sympathy with his boys. It cannot honestly be said that this is true of Arnold. For him, boyhood was an unfortunate stage in the transition between childhood and manhood, and he said bluntly that his purpose was to shorten this period of life as much as possible.[2] This elimination of boyhood was linked with the evil and temptation that developed rapidly on entry to the school and persisted for years, until in fact, the boy

[1] See p. 45.   [2] See pp. 79–83.

had acquired the spirit of manhood and could balance the tendency to be attracted by evil with a new philosophy of life and christian values. The period of waiting for this transition stage to pass was agony, and it was the duty of all masters to hasten it by persuading the young to face evil squarely, doing battle consciously on their own behalf and absorbing themselves in serious issues instead of frivolity. No wonder that the boys from Rugby were dubbed 'old before their time', and that some of them in after years bewailed their lost youth. It has to be admitted that, apart from the general aspects, Arnold never really understood the spirit of boyhood. He tried to combat the codes of boys, their lying, solidarity, and refusal to 'split' by applying adult methods, without recognising the need of boys for a society of their own with rules, loyalties and hierarchies.[1]

Arnold was a believer in the transfer of training. An education based on a narrow field did not necessarily produce narrowness but bestowed a general benefit which could be seen when the person turned to new studies and situations. To this extent the mind was a tool which could be applied in any direction provided its quality had been explored and the limits established in one direction first. It was important to stretch the mind, and to Arnold it was self-evident that the classics were best for this purpose since they were based on exciting languages, and dealt with all the faculties, and with the fundamental problems of mankind at the height of human civilisation. Arnold was therefore no innovator in the curriculum though he did insist that the classics should be taught to bring out their reasoning qualities and in particular their relevance to the

[1] This is seen in his attitude to the problems of fishing and bounds. See, for example, T. W. Bamford, *Thomas Arnold*, pp. 71–3 and note on p. 217.

English language and to modern political and social history.[1] Even so, the figures in his own account of Rugby School and reproduced here in the table below, show that the diet was very restricted. Out of a total of $28\frac{3}{4}$ teaching hours a week no less than 20 were devoted to the classics in some form or other, leavened with the history and

Weekly allocation of time per subject at Rugby about 1834.[2]

Subject	Hours per week
Classics	$17\frac{3}{4}$
History and Geography (mainly of antiquity)	$3\frac{1}{2}$
Mathematics	$2\frac{3}{4}$
French	$2\frac{3}{4}$
Scripture[3]	2
Optional[4]	
Total	$28\frac{3}{4}$

geography of antiquity and the classical side of scripture. Mathematics and French were both compulsory, and in this part of its teaching Rugby compared very favourably with other public schools of the period. At Harrow both

[1] See pp. 106–14.

[2] Source: *QJEd*, vol. VII, No. XIV, 1834, and elsewhere. In addition there was prep. Societies of all kinds existed. These and games were organised by the boys and have been omitted. There were half-holidays on Tuesday, Thursday and Saturday. Typical times for lessons for one day were (Monday): 7–8 a.m.; 9.15–11; 2.15–5 p.m.

The allocations given here do not allow for time taken in change-overs etc.

[3] The amount of time allotted was variable and much of it could be regarded as classical owing to its language and historical nature. In addition there were the regular attendances in chapel, confirmation classes, etc.

[4] Options included music, occasional lectures in natural philosophy, extra tuition, etc.

mathematics and French were relegated to options, and the compulsory studies were uncompromisingly classical.[1]

Whereas the narrow curriculum was only to be expected from other headmasters of the time, with Arnold it is somewhat surprising in a man who was anything but narrow himself. His interests and writings on industry, botany, natural science, the church, history and the social system of his own day are sufficient evidence of that. Interest, however, was one thing, education another, and he has been blamed for holding back the recognition of science and the rest of the modern curriculum. On this there are two points of importance—the first that he interpreted the classics in a very wide way stressing their logical qualities, their relationship to English and modern problems; the second that his opinion showed signs of change towards the end of his life: 'I do really think that with boys and young men, it is not right to leave them in ignorance of the beginnings of physical science. It is so hard to begin anything in after life, and so comparatively easy to continue what has been begun.'[2] That was written on 8 May 1840, two years before Arnold died. There are other indications that he was moving to a new mellowing and a new appraisal.

On the testing of the curriculum Arnold was quite prophetic. He foresaw that the increasing tempo and competition of life would result in ever increasing demands for the proper selection of personnel with a corresponding stress on examinations: 'All this *will* be certainly, and no human power can stop it.'[3]

But the new era would bring its own problems. There was a danger that examinations might grow fashionable and be extolled for their own sake. In spite of this, he

---

[1] According to one calculation for Harrow, there were $18\frac{1}{2}$ hours for classics out of $20\frac{1}{2}$, with 6 hours allowed for options.

[2] For fuller extract, see pp. 115–16. [3] See p. 117.

regarded the race for qualifications as right and just, for it would stimulate wider and deeper scholarship, help the education of girls and reflect different facets of education by their possible variety.

Even if the classical regimen had fulfilled all that was claimed for it, the fact remains that it did not really fit a young man to step into the new world of early Victoria. It is true that most boys at Rugby were well connected, many with a gentry background, and as such there was no particular financial urgency for them to work; but equally there were many who saw their future in one of the learned professions, in administration at home or overseas, or in the armed forces. It was as yet somewhat early for 'modern sides' and the whole development of vocational education at this level; but at least one would have expected a headmaster to encourage a boy to look ahead and find his niche in the future, to bolster the enthusiasm of youth, or at least to smooth the way as much as possible. In fact Arnold did the reverse, although he was entirely in favour of the professional way of life, 'without which I scarcely see how a man can live honestly'.[1] But he saw the whole business of professionalism as one of duty, a kind of moral magnet contributing to the common good. However, when it came to a consideration of individual professions, Arnold's remarks were hardly complimentary: 'moral nastiness'[2] was the phrase for lawyers; 'low morals'[3] for medical students; even work in the church was not without its difficulties since boys coming from a gentry background would find it difficult to fulfil the essential condition of being in social sympathy with the congregation.

The moral issues and the sense of duty were the stumbling block. Arnold could not square the christian ethic with

[1] See p. 149.　　　　　[2] See p. 149.
[3] See p. 117.

the practice of the professions. How could he commend the law to a boy when, although it was glorious on the one hand, it was infamous on the other, with its open and deliberate attempts to blacken character? Similarly the soldier's life and the whole concept of the hero was hardly compatible with moral virtue. If the boys really understood these dicta from the pulpit—a doubtful premise in view of his complicated style—then they must have heard these condemnations of their cherished (if temporary) goals with some puzzlement in view of the fact that the man in question was headmaster of a school whose duty it was to train the sons of leaders, many of whom were in the professions he was condemning.

One interpretation of this situation would be that Arnold could not and would not adjust his adult standards to the hopes and romantic yearnings of the young. He was certainly being uncompromisingly honest. Whether honesty provided a practical solution to the difficulty is another matter. Being honest or dishonest is hardly relevant when the young are inexperienced and cannot judge the issues for themselves, and when they get conflicting advice from masters, parents and elsewhere. Giving encouragement is hardly relevant either in this situation, since the process of encouragement is merely a device whereby the boys' general enthusiasm for life is not dampened by a fictional decision which is usually premature, since every schoolmaster knows that boys go through many ambitions before settling for one.

Not only did Arnold improve his own salary at Rugby very substantially, but, unlike all other headmasters, he improved the lot of his staff too. Teaching became a real career; there was no longer any need to eke it out with curacies. A man with a 'house' could indeed earn more than any headmaster in England outside the three major

schools (Eton, Harrow, Rugby), and that includes the
headmasters of Winchester and Shrewsbury as well. In
view of this, it is not surprising that Arnold had very little
trouble with his staff; they supported him in difficult times,
and in return he consulted them on all matters of importance, both individually and at meetings, treating them
as true colleagues with the same freedom and respect as
university dons.

On the instructional side of education Arnold was no
believer in the static view; he saw the role of the teacher
in terms of a university tutor. The teacher must be restless
of mind, continually expanding his horizons with study,
travel and research. Holidays were times to get away from
school and boys, relaxing in new experiences and pursuing
ideas in foreign parts. Scholarship was all important. He
set the example himself, as a glance at the list of his own
publications will indicate. A man must justify himself
continually, and he had no time at all for the schoolmaster
who obtained a first-class degree and lived on the strength
of it for the rest of his life. The standards he set were
difficult, but, just as he gained mastery by his own efforts,
so did the staff gain power and responsibility. On the
teachers' role in the moral aspect of education, he regarded
it as self-evident that this meant not only being *in loco
parentis*, but that it was concerned with the whole growth
of children within the christian spirit, including confirmation. The training of the ministry was invaluable for this
purpose, although possible exceptions could exist, as in
the remarkable instance of Bonamy Price. All this was
linked with Arnold's view of status. The joint schoolmaster–clergyman bestowed the minimum status of the
cloth, and this in turn ensured complete confidence from
the public in the academic competence and moral relia-
bility of the staff.[1] This confidence is the basis of all

[1] See pp. 94–6.

professionalism and he spelt out the lesson in no ambiguous way.

Arnold, the headmaster, was a controversial public figure; and this fact raised fundamental issues. Should a man in charge of boys hold strong, passionate and well known views against those of many parents, and should he be able to make these views known within the school itself at boy-level, sowing the seeds of disbelief within the family, and pitting son against father. One aim of education is to produce thinking individuals whose duty it is to examine matters critically, but there are some areas of thought in which truth is elusive and background belief important. Where is one to draw the line? In any case, is it possible for a headmaster to be a public figure and not influence boys indirectly? They are likely to read some of his articles and books out of curiosity alone. Fortunately headmasters are not usually political animals and public figures. The situation does not then arise, although the principle remains; and it was Arnold who fought for and defined the freedom of the headmaster through two main incidents involving politics in 1831 and religion in 1836.[1] He agreed that a man in his position had an overriding duty not to neglect the school, not to interfere with its prosperity and not to indoctrinate the boys—but apart from these lay the obligation of being a citizen, including, if necessary, the positive duty of helping to resolve the problems of England within his capacity. This second duty was sacred and private; there was no obligation on his part to discuss these matters with anyone; equally no one in authority had any right to question him on matters that did not directly affect the welfare of the boys or the school. Arnold was adamant about this, and although the 1831 affair passed off smoothly, the issue became far more serious after his religious denunciation of Newman in the

[1] See pp. 97–9.

28 INTRODUCTION

anonymous article of 1836.[1] In response to the subsequent
rumours he was asked officially by one of the Trustees
whether he had in fact written the offending article. He
refused to answer and said in effect, 'You may have the
right to sack me, but you certainly have no right to question
me about my private affairs.' There were two main points
in the relationship of the headmaster with the Trustees.
The first relates to the independence of the headmaster
from interference in running the school, and this was taken
for granted, although in many ways the position is illogical.
The second point concerns the independence of the headmaster to exercise his rights as a citizen, and it was here
that Arnold stood firm. He narrowly escaped the consequences, and this stand taken according to his conscience,
irrespective of the consequences, was impressive and
reminds one strongly of the independent spirit of the
early Inspectors and particularly of his son, Matthew.

In those days, teachers were an extremely varied collection of people, from the headmaster of Eton to the man
who could not read or write. Cohesion was impossible
and Arnold fought for the increased professionalism of
his own school, as we have seen, and was also concerned
with the status of the rest. Of these the middle-class school-
teachers were next in line and the only hope lay in increased respect and qualifications, with the growth of new
universities to serve their interests combined with a
national organisation:

The classical schools throughout the country have universities
[Oxford and Cambridge] to look to...But anything like local
universities...to encourage exertion at a commercial [middle
class] school, it is as yet vain to look for. Thus the business of
education is degraded: for a schoolmaster of a commercial
school, having no means of acquiring a general celebrity, is
rendered dependent on the inhabitants of his own immediate
neighbourhood;—if he offends them, he is ruined.[2]

[1] 'The Oxford Malignants', 1836.   [2] See p. 96.

This is a prophetic view, and it indicates the guide lines of true professional development. We are still a long way from this vision as regards teachers, although some of the network of university development has been achieved.

Arnold's ideal university was one that was national in scope with the function of serving the state and its institutions. The Oxford and Cambridge examples were ideal in some ways, if in need of reform, but they were also unrealistic. They were ideal in their social atmosphere, their teaching and the excellence of the pupil/tutor relationship, but they were unrealistic in that they were inadequate. They catered only for the rich and for one religious element; their intake was correspondingly limited. As long as dissenters and others were excluded, they were not national, and the business of a university was to serve the nation. These aspects are seen in his comments on Scottish universities, in his wrangles with Oxford and London, and in the middle class schoolmaster dilemma mentioned above.

SOURCES AND INFLUENCES

Arnold came into contact with at least three groups of reformers and may well have had contacts with others. These three were the religiously minded Noetics at Oriel College, Oxford; the Lake poets; and the ramifications of his own family connections, which included scientific men of research, social, moral and industrial reformers and clerics. In addition he came to know at various times a host of important individuals including refugees in this country and prominent men abroad. Above all he was extremely well read and took particular advantage of the encyclopedic approach to science, literature and current problems found in the *Edinburgh Review* and similar journals. When added together, this comprises a formidable list of possible sources and influence; yet the origin of his ideas is not simply a question of finding contacts with this person or that, however interesting the connections. Our whole knowledge of the man indicates that he was an individual, self-reliant mentally, and not the kind of person who would take over original ideas from others blindly. He was not a hermit either, but actively sought the company of others thinking in the same field for the purpose of clarification, discussion or even action. Altogether, one feels that essentially he had worked out the ideas from his favourite ancient authors and from the merest hints elsewhere. Even so, the sources of his ideas and his influence throw light not only on his religion and social framework, but also and especially on his educational interests.

Arnold himself placed his religious ideas firmly in the past: 'The "Idea" of my life...is the perfecting the "idea" of the Edward the Sixth Reformers,—the constructing a truly national Christian Church, and a truly national and Christian system of education.'[1] With this go the views of Richard Hooker (1553–1600) and Joseph Butler (1692–1752). These ideas were reflected in his own day by the Noetics, of whom Davison and Whately were the chief influences, although Hawkins played an important part, especially in his personal friendship, and Hampden indirectly, since he was the main target of Newman and his followers. How much Arnold owed to them in his original thinking it is difficult to say, but certainly he was a protégé of Whately well before he (Arnold) was twenty.

   Behind the Noetics, and one who is reckoned the pioneer of the Broad Church Movement, stood S. T. Coleridge, the uncle of one of Arnold's closest friends at

[1] See p. 156.

Oxford. Indeed, if a trigger were needed to explain the radical direction of Arnold's religious views—and it must be remembered that he had determined to enter the church at the age of ten—then there is little need to look further than Coleridge. The stability of the bible in the face of criticism, the church–state relationships, its national character and social involvement—all these are to be found in both Coleridge and Arnold, and they obviously have significant by-products on the educational side. How much of this was due directly to Coleridge and how much to his own original thinking it is now impossible to say, but Arnold himself acknowledged the debt and certainly to have thought out these points for himself before going to Oxford (at sixteen) would have been precociousness of a high order. In his early years, too, there were many people who attracted considerable publicity like John Bowdler, Wilberforce and Hannah More, all complaining bitterly of the onslaught of irreligion, and demanding a counter-revolution. They preached a high-sounding gospel which may well have had an effect on a serious, growing boy susceptible to religious influence. After the early period Arnold was not the only one to write on these lines; others, like W. W. Hull, had the same broad programme in the twenties and thirties.

The origin of many of his educational thoughts must be sought in religion. These include the equating of morals with religion; the concept of evil in school and its connection with original and acquired sin, together with their logical derivations; the elimination of the stage of youth; and the production of adult behaviour attitudes in the young. The same applies to his view of corporal punishment and particularly of expulsion, which became a duty, almost a holy command, stern and based directly on the authority of the bible. There are resemblances here to Whately, especially in attitudes to work and idleness, and to Hawkins. Similarly there is his bitter opponent, J. H. Newman, whose educational ideas had much in common with Arnold, not to mention other prominent headmasters of the time, all of them in orders, and many, like Butler, Moberly and Knox carrying out their own versions of christian education.

Arnold's attitude to the clergyman–schoolmaster as a curator of morals, with its implications of status, was not new, but is in line with the long English tradition linking education and religion. He did, however, carry the issue further, to its logical, financial and cultural consequence, making Rugby a school which, as far as the staff were concerned, could be compared to Harrow and particularly Eton. Important though this is for Rugby, nonetheless there was no new principle involved. Yet the background is not entirely clear, and this represents a field which may well repay further study.

Arnold's view of religion and morals is connected with his prudish ideas on the protection of youth from evil. These stem from Thomas Bowdler (who lived in the Isle of Wight for a period and was a distant relative by marriage) and Mrs Trimmer, among others, and are a reaction against Rousseau and certain aspects of the French revolution. In a similar way his religious outlook affected his view of Dickens and other popular writers as frivolous and distracting for youth.

Arnold's significance in the Broad Church Movement had an important educational by-product, for as the movement gathered strength, so did his stature and reputation rise, and his prominence certainly helped the cult of the public school headmaster. His 'missed' bishoprics are certainly among the first of the wave of promotions that came to be offered to the heads of the main four or five schools—Butler and Longley are others. The expectation of high office became so common that these headmasters could almost rely on promotion in due course, as of right. This is, in truth, a very complicated story (involving the exceptional cases of Eton and Westminster) but there is no doubt that Arnold helped to establish an elite in a select circle of posts. Once that was done, with the elevation of these men to higher and higher office, even to Canterbury in several cases, then the significance of Arnoldian-type religion and the whole policy of the church as one major element of the dual system in education can be seen as the logical development of public school dominance in English state-education even at the present day. Certainly Arnold was one of the first to be taken seriously as a man of the world who could translate easily from the headmaster's chair to other significant posts in society.

Arnold's social radicalism was based on the free man concept of the ancient world with its political, educational and responsibility overtones. This was linked inevitably with slavery in its ancient context and in the new with Clarkson and Wilberforce. Crucial to these problems are the questions of population, colonisation, industrialisation and also the implications of the French and American revolutions. This amalgam produced Arnold's first serious thoughts of which we have documentary evidence—a publication on colonisation before he was twenty.[1] There the main thought lines are indicated, if only by inference, long before he came to know and appreciate any prominent people specialising in this field. The eminence of some of these latter-day advisers must not blind us to the fact that their influence must have been secondary. A typical case is Wordsworth. Here the stress on the importance of religion and morals in social life, and the desirability of a continuous growing together of the social classes, are part

[1] 'The Effects of Distant Colonization on the Parent State', 1815.

of the affinity between the two men; it no doubt played a role in their friendship and conversation. In the same way it is easy to romanticise on the similarities of outlook of his distant relative, John Cartwright, but very little evidence of any actual influence has come to light as yet. Apart from his relatives and close friends, Arnold knew and studied the work of many other men of his time: Malthus, Owen, Ingles, Bentham, Attwood, Slaney, Wakefield, Cobbett, at least. One can even find common friends, acquaintances or correspondents among many of these, but the fact remains that we are still ignorant of any significant details. The same is true of that other question mark—the urge to form a society to investigate major social problems in a manner resembling that suggested by Francis Place. Arnold's journeys in pursuit of this quest in the midlands and the north remind us both of the terrain and the ideas and objectives he had in common with men like Oastler and Fielden among others.

The force of Arnold's social ideas relied on his personality; and it was almost inevitable, with his gentry and establishment connections, that they died with him. They have, indeed, been largely forgotten, even by scholars. Remnants, however, are certainly to be seen in Frederick Temple and other social-churchmen, and particularly in his son, Matthew, while the socio-educational field was carried on in part by Thomas Hughes and his circle.

The educational aspects of Arnold's religious and social ideas have already been mentioned. Compared with these the remainder of his educational thoughts seem trivial and traditional, even reactionary.

His belief in the faculties and his faith in the classics and classics teaching, which he related to Gabell, are part of the main stream of the educational thought of his time. His views on discipline are connected with economics and the need to establish and control the school community. Such rationalisations were old, even then, and his own views on some of the situations at Rugby (some of which are reproduced later) read, in the light of memoirs and the accounts of his own actions, as though he were out of touch with events.

The policy of breeding responsibility and leadership within the structure of the school community was already established in many boarding schools before Arnold went to Rugby, and, indeed, this provided the whole basis for their theory of leisure, and the corresponding development of individuality and manliness, as inherited from the eighteenth century. Even the concept of the school as a republic, a self-governing organisation, has parallels in other schools of the time, at Eton in part, but particularly in the work of the Hill family. Arnold certainly knew the Hills and must have read about the family indirectly, but there is no proven connection and influence. Arnold, of course, borrowed the corporate self-governing idea straight from Plato and Aristotle (he even alludes to it himself) but the whole concept was common at the time and is seen typically in Lytton Bulwer. Even so, it would be stretching the point too far to say that Arnold considered this to be a major principle (in spite of his writings on the subject), for he was not really concerned with the socialising aspect of boys' education in the Rugby setting. Indeed, he was convinced that, apart from the important business of making useful friends, a private education was superior in many ways to that at a public boarding school. The background to his support for private education lies partly in his character, partly in the moral issues, but also in its proven worth historically through the gentry tradition.

Arnold's view of the middle-class teacher and middle-class education arose from his thoughts about the public school tradition of the teacher–clergyman. The need to develop this particular middle-class aspect rested on the exploitation of foundations (themselves ancient in origin) and on his concept of the local university and the mass production of graduates, for which he had Scottish parallels in mind and to some extent too the technological background of England, Scotland and the continent. It is a great pity that on this highly important issue there is not enough available material for us to be sure of all the details, although the relationship of these ideas to those of his son, Matthew, and son-in-law, Forster, are evident. As for lower-class education, he visualised at least the same responsibilities and development as did the early social reformers since these were necessary concomitants for lower-class power.

On the role of the headmaster Arnold consolidated the position already gained by the old heads of Eton and Westminster as exemplified by Busby, and even by one of his old teachers, Gabell. However, he defined the position more clearly, spelt out conflicting areas of interest, and related it to ideas of the state and citizenship. Although theoretically important and a milestone of professional status, this was a stand of limited practical significance, benefiting only the rare, unique figure of the Frederick Temple stamp. On staff meetings and staff independence Arnold is again true to his ancient world and to university tradition. This kind of group control and discussion is seen elsewhere and indeed, for schools, has always been an essential feature of the 'college' type of institution.

Arnold's influence on education, especially that of public schools, was immense, though whether the reputation was justified and how far it was related to his own work and to that of his disciples, the reader must make up his own mind from the evidence presented both here and elsewhere.

In spite of everything he did, Arnold still remains a lonely and misunderstood figure. The present book at least attempts to present some of his own educational thoughts in his own words.

ARNOLD'S METHOD OF WRITING[1]

A page of one of Arnold's letters gives the impression of a rapid but steady filling up of the available space. The writing is clear, easy to read and distinctive, spreading downwards in neatly spaced rows on both sides of the paper, except for occasional gaps in the middle at the sides, and due allowance for the address. The words and phraseology are essentially modern with only the slightest touch of the eighteenth century. Nouns invariably begin with a capital letter; spellings and particularly punctuation are quaint at times by modern arbitrary standards, while the short last lines at the end of paragraphs are continued with a thin pen to the edge of the sheet to indicate a closure of the argument or that there was no more he wished to say on that particular theme. On the rare occasions when the paper ran out, he would turn the sheet through a right angle and continue the flow as before in neat lines across the original writing to produce a lattice, criss-cross effect that is still readable if a little confusing.[2] This overall neatness persisted as a distinctive feature from the early days until the last few years, when the first signs of untidiness and disturbance begin to appear.

Not only was he neat, but he rarely made a slip or mistake. In all the mass of manuscripts examined, the

[1] For a list of Thomas Arnold's works, see the Bibliography, pp. 175–6.

[2] Mary Arnold was addicted even more to this procedure of covering the same surface twice. See her letters in the Brotherton Library, Leeds.

number of corrections can almost be counted on one hand. Once written, he very rarely went over the work again and was not really concerned with niceties of style. This apparent fact is obvious to anyone who has studied and compared his letters and printed works, but is somewhat surprising in view of his emphasis upon the use of the correct style in Latin or Greek translation, and his insistence upon finding the exact words to suit the passages under discussion. Apparently he felt no urge to polish the words and arguments in an attempt to seek the final form of the message, and, as they were committed to paper at first thought, so they remained in the final version. One natural consequence is the constancy of his style. Only minor differences show themselves between his letters, his sermons and his other published works. The rapid conversational style which suited him, meant that arguments were frequently interspersed with interesting if irrelevant digressions. With few exceptions, chiefly in the religious field, the printed pages do not present Arnold's ideas in any concentrated form; and we have to gather material for related themes from a variety of sources. This failure to link and connect is undoubtedly related to the lack of revision. Yet it is puzzling; most writers find it quite compulsive. It is difficult to believe that Arnold's standards of appreciation were low or that he was easy to please—more likely he was impatient and his mind had already passed on to more urgent things. Certainly his life was busy, and there was little enough time to tidy up the ends of work already done. He rarely gave titles to his works, and even the evocative heading of the anti-Newman article in the *Edinburgh Review* was chosen by someone else.[1] Arnold's eldest daughter indicates some of these points in her Preface to the collected edition of the *Sermons:*

[1] 'The Oxford Malignants', 1836.

My Father's (Sermons) were written in the midst of a busy life, almost invariably on a Sunday afternoon, in the couple of hours before he went into chapel, and are therefore no elaborate productions, but direct practical addresses to the congregation before him...the titles, both of the volumes and of the separate Sermons, are for the most part not of the author's own giving; the only volume named by himself is the fourth...and the only Sermons he named are those in the volume entitled 'Christian Life and Doctrine'.[1]

Arnold was not a cautious writer. If he felt strongly, as he often did, then the words matched his mood. When he felt outraged the denunciation is fierce; when he was despondent the spirit is one of despair. His friends often cautioned him on this point, knowing that he could rush and commit himself to paper in the first flush of outrage, expressing views which were ill-considered and conveying a totally false impression. It is not difficult to find such extremes in the 'Oxford Malignants', his writings on social reform, and particularly in some of the Sermons, where the feeling is sometimes matched by that passionate delivery from the pulpit which struck some of the more sensitive boys.

Arnold had a large circle of friends and part of each evening at home was usually set aside for writing personal letters, which were then addressed and folded in the form of the period. Although the bulk was done in the evening and in the holidays, he hated to waste time and often used to write letters in class while the boys were engaged in set work.

Arnold had an immense output—letters, diaries, sermons, histories, articles, religious and classical books. He was

---

[1] *Christian Life*. Sermons, preached mostly in the village church at Laleham, by Thomas Arnold (volume 1 of the 1878 edition). Preface by the Editor (J.M.F. = Jane Forster, née Arnold). The last volume mentioned in the quotation is the third volume of the 1878 edition, first published in 1834.

always writing, even on holidays. He was interested, if critical, about everything but music, and had the urge to set it all down while it was fresh in the mind. At the same time it is difficult not to believe that he found in writing a compulsive release, with a certain therapeutic value. He passed out through his pen his hopes, fears, feelings, ideas. He seemed to need a positive outlet for expressing these views over and above the printed word. The fact that he had already written about and published his thoughts on a particular point did not satisfy him—he seemed compelled to go on reproducing the same arguments time and time again to different correspondents, even to the use of the same phrases.

NOTE ON THE SELECTIONS MADE
IN THIS WORK

Arnold wrote only three articles on education. One on Rugby School and the teaching of the classics,[1] the second on discipline,[2] and the third on the nature of knowledge.[3] These are interesting but in no way remarkable. The rest of his work, including the more fundamental things he had to say on education, are scattered over six volumes of sermons, letters to newspapers and letters to friends. They are hardly ideal vehicles for the analysis of values and of educational problems in depth, since the letters are personal and the sermons were designed for declamatory, often emotional, occasions from the pulpit to successive generations of boys. A further problem arises in the complex view Arnold took of education. He saw it dovetailed within population problems, social theory, politics, religious and academic considerations. Some indication of this complexity has already been given. Many passages where the theme for example is mainly sociological, or is only marginally concerned with education, or has educational overtones which only the most patient reader can discern have here been omitted. It remains true that any final insight into Arnold's ideas on education can only be obtained from a scrutiny of the whole output; there is no substitute for this. To have adopted such an approach would not have been practicable for our purposes here. Selections have been drawn from a very wide coverage of writings—some of the extracts being necessarily very short. The selections have been arranged under

[1] 'Rugby School', *QJEd*, vol. VII, No. XIV (1834).
[2] 'On the Discipline of the Public Schools', *QJEd*, vol. IX, No. XVIII (1835).
[3] 'On the Divisions and Mutual Relations of Knowledge', 1839.

themes, and each extract (or two or three extracts in some cases) has been given a brief explanatory heading to help the reader. These headings have been printed in italics. Indeed we follow the tradition established by earlier Arnold editors; for, as we have seen, this author provided few titles for his own works.

In many places passages have been omitted because they are digressions from the theme Arnold is discussing. No indication of these omissions is given so that the text may be read more easily. There are, however, full references to sources at the end of each passage.

The notes on the text may be found on pp. 167–8.

WRITINGS ON
EDUCATION

EDUCATION AND THE SOCIAL
CLASSES

PUBLIC-SCHOOL EDUCATION

Public-school education; the value of historical connections and size; school traditions

The advantages of great places of education are very considerable, and the benefits of such foundations as ours impose a great responsibility on all of us. I said the advantages of *great* places of education; and I meant to lay a stress upon the epithet. It seems to me that there is, or ought to be, something very ennobling in being connected with any establishment at once ancient and magnificent: where all about us, and all the associations belonging to the objects around us, should be great, splendid and elevating. What an individual ought, and often does, derive, from the feeling that he is born of an old and illustrious race, from being familiar, from his childhood, with the walls and with the trees that speak of the past no less than of the present, and make both full of images of greatness,— this in an inferior degree belongs to every member of an ancient and celebrated place of education. In this respect every one has a responsibility imposed upon him, which I wish that we more considered. We know how school traditions are handed down from one school generation to another; and what is it, if in all these there shall be nothing great, nothing distinguished, nothing but a record, to say the best of it, of mere boyish amusements, when it is not a record of boyish follies? Every generation, in which a low and foolish spirit prevails, does its best to pollute the local influences of the place; to degrade its associations, to deprive the thought of belonging to it of anything that may enkindle and ennoble the minds of those who come after. And if these foolish or tame associations continue, they make the evil worse; persons who appreciate highly the elevating effect of a great and ancient foundation, will no longer send their sons to a place which has forfeited one of its most valuable powers; whose antiquity has nothing of the dignity, nothing of the romance of antiquity, but is either a blank, or worse than a blank. In smaller schools one cannot look forward to posterity; when our children are of an age to commence their education, a total change may have taken place in the spot, and all its associations may have vanished for ever. But here it is not so; the size, the scale, the wealth of a great institution like this ensures its permanency, so far as anything on earth is permanent. The good and the evil, the nobleness or the vileness, which may exist on this ground now, will live and breathe here in the days of our children. [*Sermons*, vol. 3, pp. 137–8.]

Boarding education and the effects of living away from home.
The advantages of being a day-boy at boarding school

You are absent from home so large a portion of the year, that other persons and other objects engross, of necessity, a large share of your thoughts and feelings. The absence, certainly, you cannot help; but you may help increasing its natural effect by your own conduct. You become ashamed of speaking of your homes and relations in the natural language of a good heart; you talk of them to one another as affording you such and such enjoyments; and you are ashamed if it appears that other boys have greater liberty, and are more indulged at home than yourselves. And this extends to school also: you do not like to have less money than other boys—to have fewer presents sent you—to find your friends more unwilling to pay your debts, than the friends of other boys are to pay theirs. This not only interferes with your pleasures, but hurts your pride; and I believe that the annoyance to your pride is very often what you mind the most. Thus talking, and thus feeling towards home, the effect of long absence is increased tenfold; concealment and restraint are sometimes the dispositions with which you meet your fathers; you do not like to tell them all that you have done; and you think yourselves hardly used if your requests have not been all complied with. In this undutiful and unchildlike temper, the period which you spend at home is too short to soften you. You return again to school, and the mischief rapidly increases; and it too often happens, that when you go from school to college, the evil becomes yet worse; extravagance there is practised on a larger scale, and is often accompanied with other vices, which make confidence toward a parent still more difficult. Then comes actual life, and you go to other parts of the world, or settle at a distance from your father's house: the opportunities of undoing the bad and cold impressions of early life are no more attainable; and all that passes between father and son is a few letters, and a few short visits, till the son is called on to perform his last act of duty, in following his father's body to the grave.

Far, very far, am I from saying or thinking that this is always, or even generally the case to the full extent: but it is the tendency of schools to produce such a state of things. Yet so catching is this shame, that I am afraid even those boys among you, who have the happiness of being at once both at school and at home, are tempted to throw away their advantages. The situation of those boys I have always thought most fortunate—with all the opportunities of forming lasting friendships with those of their own age which a public school so largely affords, and with the opportunity also of keeping up all their home affections, of never losing that lively interest in all that is said and done under their father's roof, which an absence of several months cannot fail, in some measure, to chill. Your fault then is by so much the greater, if you make yourselves strangers to domestic feelings and affections, through your own fault; if you think you have any dearer friendships, or any that can better become either youth or manhood, than those which God Himself has marked out for you in your own homes. Add others to them if you will, and it is your wisdom and your duty to do so; but beware how you let any less sacred connection weaken the solemn and universal bond of domestic love. [*Sermons*, vol. 2, pp. 60–1.]

Choosing the best kind of education: public school v. private tutor

Experience seems to point out no one plan of education as decidedly the best; it only says, I think, that public education (public schools) is the best where it answers. But then the question is, will it answer with one's own boy? and if it fails, is not the failure complete? It becomes a question of particulars: a very good private tutor would tempt me to try private education, or a very good public school, with connections amongst the boys at it, might induce me to venture upon public. Still there is much chance in the matter: for a school may change its character greatly, even with the same master, by the prevalence of a good or bad set of boys; and this no caution can guard against. But I should certainly advise anything rather than a private school of above thirty boys. Large private schools, I think, are the worst possible system: the choice lies between public schools, and an education whose character may be strictly private and domestic. [*SL*, XCVIII, 15 April 1835 p. 358.]

Public schools as the nurseries of vice

'Public schools,' he [John Bowdler] says, 'are the very seats and nurseries of vice. It may be unavoidable, or it may not; but the fact is indisputable. None can pass through a large school without being pretty intimately acquainted with vice; and few, alas! very few, without tasting too largely of that poisoned bowl. The hour of grace and repentance at length arrives, and they are astonished at their former fatuity. The young convert looks back with inexpressible regret to those hours which have been wasted in folly, or worse than folly; and the more lively his sense of the newly discovered mercies, the more piercing his anguish for past indulgences.'

Now, although too many of us may not be able to join in the last part of this description, yet we must all, I think, be able to bear witness to the truth of the first part. I am afraid the fact is, indeed, indisputable—'Public schools *are* the very seats and nurseries of vice.' But he goes on to say, 'It may be unavoidable or it may not'; and these words seem to me as though they ought to fill us with the deepest shame of all. For what a notion does it give, that we should have been so long and so constantly bad, that it may be doubted whether our badness be not unavoidable—whether we are not evil hopelessly and incurably. And this to be true of places which were intended to be seats of Christian education.

But, it may be asked, what is meant when public schools are called 'the seats and nurseries of vice?' That is properly a nursery of vice, where a boy unlearns the pure and honest principles which he may have received at home, and gets, in their stead, others which are utterly low, and base, and mischievous; where he loses his modesty, his respect for truth, and his affectionateness, and becomes coarse, and false, and unfeeling. That, too, is a nursery of vice and most fearfully so, where vice is bold, and forward, and presuming, and goodness is timid and shy, and existing as if by sufferance,—where the good, instead of setting the tone of society, and branding with disgrace those who disregard it, are themselves exposed to reproach for their goodness, and shrink before the open avowal of evil principles, which the bad are striving to make the law of the community. That is a nursery of vice where the restraints laid upon evil are considered as so much taken from liberty, and where, generally speaking, evil is more willingly screened and concealed than detected and punished.

Now, then, to what is this owing? Public schools are made up of the very same persons whom we have known, a few years earlier, to be pure-minded and obedient children,—whom we know, a few years later, to be at least decent and useful men. What especial cloud hangs over this one part of our life's current, that the stream here will ever run dark and sullen, while on its earlier and its later course it is either all bright and lively, or the impurity of its waters is lost to the distant view in the breadth and majesty of their volume? I must touch upon the causes, or how shall we be able to point out the remedies.

Unquestionably, the time of life at which you are arrived, and more particularly the younger boys among you, is in itself, exceedingly dangerous. It is just the time, beyond all others in life, when temptation is great, and the strength of character to resist it exceedingly small. This makes you unapt and unwilling to think; and he who does not think, must surely do one of two things,—he must submit himself entirely to be guided by the advice and direction of others, like young children, or else he must certainly go wrong. Another cause is, that at no place or time of life are people so much the slaves of custom as boys at school. If a thing has been an old practice, be it ever so mischievous, ever so unworthy, it is continued without scruple; if a thing is new, be it ever so useful and ever so excellent, it is apt to be regarded as a grievance.

The question which boys seem to ask, is not, What ought we to be, and what may the school become, if we do our duty?—but, What have we been used to, and is the school as good as it was formerly? Old habits, old practices, are handed down from generation to generation, and, above all, old feelings. Now it is certain that education, like everything else, was not brought to perfection when our great schools were first founded: the system required a great deal to make it what it ought to be. I am afraid that Christian principles were not enough brought forward, that lower motives were encouraged, and a lower standing altogether suffered to prevail. The system also was too much one of fear and outward obedience; the obedience of the heart and the understanding were little thought of. And the consequence has been the same in every old school in England,—that boys have learnt to regard themselves and their masters as opposites to one another, as having two distinct interests; it being the master's object to lay on restrictions, and abridge their liberty, while it was their business, by all sorts of means,— combination amongst themselves, concealment, trick, open falsehood, or open disobedience,—to baffle his watchfulness, and escape his severity. It cannot be too strong to say, that this is at least the case, so far as regards the general business of schools: the boys' interest and pleasure are supposed to consist in contriving to have as little work as they can, the master's in putting on as much as he can; —a strange and sad state of feeling, which must have arisen, I fear from the habit of keeping out of sight the relation in which we both stand, masters and boys alike, to our common Master in heaven, and that it is His service which we all have, after our several stations, to labour in. [*Sermons*, vol. 2, pp. 80–5.]

The rapid pollution of new boys at a public boarding school[1]

Some of you, [boys at Rugby School] at least, and I hope very many, have had the blessing of good parents at home; you have been taught to hear of God and of Christ, to say your prayers, and to remember that wherever you are, and whatever you are doing, God ever sees you. You have seen in your own house nothing base, nothing cruel, nothing ill-natured, and especially nothing false. You thought a lie was one of the most hateful things in the world; and that to give up to your brothers and sisters, and to please your parents, was a great deal better than to be always quarrelling and envying, and to think of pleasing no one but yourselves. I hope and believe that many of you, before you came to school, were thus taught, and that the teaching was not in vain; that you not only heard of what was good, but, on the whole, practised it.

But how is it with you now? I am afraid that I dare not ask those who have been here so much as one half year or more: but even if I were to ask those who have not yet been here so much as one month, what sort of an answer could you give, if you answered truly? Do you think of God *now*? Do you remember that He ever, and in every place, sees what you are doing? Do you say your prayers to Him? Do you still think that lying, and all those shuffling, dishonest excuses, which are as bad as lying, are base, and contemptible, and wicked?—or have you heard these things so often from others, even if you yourselves have not been guilty of them, that you think there cannot be any great harm in them? Do you still love to be kind to your companions, never teasing or ill-treating them, and never being ill-natured and out of temper with them?—or have you already been accustomed to the devilish pleasure of giving pain to others: and whilst you are yourselves teased and ill-used by some who are stronger than you, do you repeat the very same conduct to those who are weaker than you? Are you still anxious to please your parents; and, in saying your lessons, do you still retain the natural thought of a well-bred and noble disposition, that you would like to say them as well as you can, and to please those who teach you?—or have you already learnt the first lesson in the devil's school to laugh at what is good, and generous, and high-principled, and to be ashamed of doing your duty?

Now if you have been wholly or in part corrupted in these points, within one short month, so that the good learnt in ten or twelve years has been overthrown in less than thirty days;—and if this has happened not to one or two only, who might happen to be weak, and easily led into evil, but, more or less, to all of you, and in a greater degree, generally speaking, to those who have been here for a longer period; if, in short, you all find that you would be afraid to speak and act just as you ought to do, because you would be laughed at and disliked if you did;—then you have already had some experience of the truth of what the Bible tells us, that man's nature is corrupt and bad. It shows you plainly, how strong must be our evil disposi-tions, when you see them, in so short a time, getting the better of those that have had ten or twelve years to ripen; it shows you, too, how much the world is opposed to God. Every boy brings some good with him, at least, from home, as well as some evil; and yet you see how very much more catching the evil is than the good, or else you would make one another better by mixing together; and if any single boy did anything wrong, it would be condemned by the general opinion of all the school, just as some wrong things, such as stealing money, for example, are condemned at present. [*Sermons*, vol. 2, pp. 33–5.]

MIDDLE-CLASS EDUCATION

The instructional curriculum of the schools; professional and liberal education. The need for later leaving and the need of 'liberal' education as a necessity for modern society

I believe it often happens, that boys in the lowest form of a commercial school require absolutely to be taught to read. They have been neglected at home in their earliest years, till, when they come to eleven or twelve years of age, their friends find themselves obliged to send them to school; forgetting, however, that owing to their own neglect, what ought to be the work of seven or eight years has now to be completed as it can within three or four. But supposing a boy able to read and write, his education, properly so called, then commences. He receives instruction in arithmetic, history, and geography; in English grammar, and in composition. The rudiments of physical science, carried on to a greater or less degree of advancement, are also taught him; and with a view to his particular business in life, he learns land surveying, if he is to be brought up in agricultural pursuits; or book-keeping if he is intended for trade. His religious instruction varies probably more than anything else, according to the personal character of his instructor, the line of study here being much less clearly marked out, except to a man who is himself in earnest as to its importance. Sometimes the boys are required to analyse grammatically any sentence in an English book, and to give the derivations of the several words in it, just as boys at classical schools are called upon to do in Greek and Latin. And doubtless there may be many commercial schools, especially in the manufacturing districts, where the course of study far surpasses what is here given, and where the instruction on scientific subjects, in chemistry, and in mechanics, is carried to a high degree of proficiency.

But I confess that this is not the point upon which I feel much anxiety. I have little doubt that boys will be sufficiently taught all that they require for their particular calling; and scientific knowledge is so generally valued, and confers a power so immediately felt, that I think its diffusion may safely be reckoned on. This, however, has nothing to do with the knowledge which the Reform Bill calls for. A man may be ever so good a chemist, or ever so good a mechanic, or ever so good an engineer, and yet not at all the fitter to enjoy the elective franchise. And if we call a people educated who possess only scientific or physical knowledge, we practically misapply the term; for though such knowledge be a very good education, as far as a man's trade or livelihood is concerned, yet, in a political sense, and as a qualification for the exercise of political power, it is no education at all. The distinction requires to be stated more fully.

Every man, from the highest to the lowest, has two businesses; the one his own particular profession or calling, be it what it will, whether that of soldier, seaman, farmer, lawyer, mechanic, labourer, &c.—the other his general calling, which he has in common with all his neighbours, namely, the calling of a citizen and a man. The education which fits him for the first of these two businesses, is called professional; that which fits him for the second, is called liberal. But because every man must do this second business, whether he does it well or ill, so people are accustomed to think that it is learnt more easily. A man who has learnt it indifferently seems, notwithstanding, to get through life with tolerable comfort; he may be thought not to be very wise or very agreeable, yet he manages to get married, and to bring up a family, and to mix in society with his friends and neighbours. Whereas, a man who has learnt his other business indifferently, I mean, his particular trade or calling, is in some danger of starving outright. People will not employ an indifferent workman when good ones are to be had in plenty; and, therefore, if he has learnt his particular business badly, it is likely that he will not be able to practise it at all.

Thus it is, that while ignorance of a man's special business is instantly detected, ignorance of his great business as a man and a citizen is scarcely noticed, because there are so many who share in it. Thus we see everyone ready to give an opinion about politics, or about religion, or about morals, because it is said these are every man's business. And so they are, and if people would learn them as they do their own particular business, all would do well: but never was the proverb more fulfilled which says that every man's business is no man's. It is worse indeed than if it were no man's; for now it is every man's business to meddle in, but no man's to learn. And this general ignorance does not make itself felt directly,—if it did, it were more likely to be remedied: but the process is long and round about; false notions are entertained and acted upon; prejudices and passions multiply; abuses become manifold; difficulty and distress at last press on the whole community; whilst the same ignorance which produced the mischief now helps to confirm it or to aggravate it, because it hinders them from seeing where the root of the whole evil lay, and sets them upon some vain attempt to correct the consequences, which they never think of curing, because they do not suspect the cause.

I believe it is generally the case, at least in the agricultural districts, that a boy is taken away from school at fourteen. He is taken away, less than half educated, because his friends want him to enter upon his business in life without any longer delay. That is, the interests of his great business as a man are sacrificed to the interest of his particular business as a farmer or a tradesman. And yet very likely the man who cares so little about political knowledge, is very earnest about political power, and thinks that it is most unjust if he has no share in the election of the members of the legislature. I do not blame any one for taking his son from school at an early age when he is actually obliged to do so, but I fear that in too many instances there is no sense entertained of the value of education, beyond its fitting a boy for his own immediate business in life: and until this be altered for the better, I do not see that we are likely to grow much wiser, or that though political power may pass into different hands, that it will be exercised more purely or sensibly than it has been.

'But the newspapers—they are cheap and ready instructors in political knowledge, from whom all may, and all are willing to learn.' But *we* know, and every honest man connected with a newspaper would confess also, that our instruction is often worse than useless to him who has never had any other. We suppose that our readers have some knowledge and some principles of their own; and adapt our language to them accordingly. I am afraid that we in many cases suppose this untruly; and the wicked amongst our fraternity make their profit out of their readers' ignorance, by telling them that they are wise. But instruction must be regular and systematic; whereas a newspaper must give the facts of the day or the week,—and if it were to overload these with connected essays upon general principles, it would not be read. Real knowledge, like every thing else of the highest value, is not to be obtained so easily. It must be worked for,—studied for,—thought for,—and more than all, it must be prayed for. And that is education, which lays the foundation of such habits,—and gives them, so far as a boy's early age will allow, their proper exercise. For doing this, the materials exist in the studies actually pursued in our commercial schools; but it cannot be done effectually, if a boy's education is to be cut short at fourteen. His *schooling* indeed may be ended without mischief, if his parents are able to guide his *education* afterwards; and the way to gain this hereafter, is to make the most of the schooling time of the rising generation,—that finding how much may be done even in their case, within the limited time allowed for their education, they may be anxious to give *their* children greater advantages, that the fruit may be proportionably greater.

It may be that this is impracticable, to which I have only to say that I will not believe it to be so till I am actually unable to hope otherwise; for if it be impracticable, my expectations of good from any political changes are faint indeed. [*MW*, pp. 231–5. For teachers in middle-class schools, see pp. 94–7.]

LOWER-CLASS EDUCATION

Education of the poor is not education since the leaving age is too low

Many persons confound reading and writing with education: they consider themselves as having been engaged in educating the poor; and then, when they see that their labours have produced little fruit, they are half bewildered when they hear it said that this is a plain proof that to educate the poor can do no good. In that sense of the word I know of no provision hitherto made in England for the education of the poor, nor, perhaps, is it possible that any can be made. I never knew any poor man who could properly be said to be educated; except, in some rare circumstances, where men, breaking through all difficulties, have, by their own power of mind and indefatigable industry, succeeded in educating themselves. If we [the parents of public school children] call our own children educated at the age when we commonly send them to school for the first time, if their education is completed at eight or nine years old,—then may we call those educated who have been taught to read and write at our parish schools. But if reading and writing are not education, but the mere preparatory steps to it,—then to talk of the education of the poor, is to talk of a thing which does not exist; and to expect an important moral and religious improvement from the machinery now in operation, is to look for a full crop of corn after sowing a single handful of seed. He who has a high sense of what education really is, and how grievously the poor stand in need of it, will feel that if the mere first steps to it have been found useful, the reality itself, which it is his bounden duty to try to introduce, may well be looked to as a source of still greater blessings. [*Sermons*, vol. 2, pp. 264–6. For religious education and lower-class schools, see pp. 68–72.]

Neither the nature of the instruction given at what are called English schools, nor the time that any workman can spend at them, are such as to give him much moral and political knowledge. Or, are they to get this knowledge in after life from newspapers? Do newspapers pretend, or is it their business, to give a general view of the principles of any science? To tell us of past times, or of the state of foreign countries? It is true, they give us an account of passing events in other countries, but they cannot do more. [*MW*, p. 204. See also *Sermons*, vol. 5, pp. 86–8, for 'Education and Instruction'.]

How can a poor man find time to be educated? You may establish schools, but he will not have time to attend them, for a few years of early boyhood are no more enough to give education, than the spring months can do the summer's work when the summer is all cold and rainy. [Stanley, *Travelling Journal*, 20 July 1841, pp. 763–4.]

The limitations and strength of education based on book instruction and the weakness of education given by the Mechanics' Institutes

Knowledge is the material for the mind to work upon; but if the instrument be blunt or out of order, what avails the fineness of the material? it continues stuff unwrought and useless. Further, we shall have seen that education in the proper sense of the word cannot be given equally to a great number of persons. You may teach them the formal sciences indeed equally, so that their reasoning powers may be cultivated alike; but you cannot do the same with their judgement or their power of combination. For the judgement depending greatly on a knowledge of men, and the power of combination increasing with the number of ideas presented to it, they who by circumstances are confined to a limited sphere, who see little variety, who have never associated with many highly cultivated minds, and above all with minds cultivated under different circumstances of rank, profession, and country, must labour under disadvantages which no mere book instruction can remove. But at the same time it is important to see how much mere book instruction can do, if it be applied wisely. If we read the works of great men, philosophers, or orators, poets, historians, or divines, the works of great men, whose own views are large and profound, whose minds have combined actively a great variety of ideas, and beautifully expressed them; and if we read them with our minds alive and awake to catch and to understand, we are not only, as has been often remarked, in a better society than is easily to be found amongst living men, but we gain a far wider and truer experience of men and of things than is gained often-times by a whole life of active intercourse with what is called the world. And not to speak of foreign writers, what a treasure of wisdom and of experience is to be gained from the works of Bacon, his Essays and his Advancement of Learning; from the conversation of Johnson as recorded by Boswell, far more indeed than from his writings; from the Aids to Reflection, and the Literary Remains of Coleridge, from the Sermons of Butler; from the poetry of Milton and of Shakespeare. Only let us read with a mind attentive and inquiring; let us for instance always acquaint ourselves with the age in which the writer lived, with something of the circumstances of his life and the peculiarities of his character. And when I speak of the age in which he lived, I do not speak of a knowledge of a mere date, which is good for nothing; as for instance that Bacon was born in 1560, and died in 1626; but an idea of what that period was, what events Bacon saw, and with what men he held intercourse, how remote from, or how like to our own. An inquiring spirit is not a presumptuous one, but the very contrary: He whose whole recorded life was intended to be our perfect example, is described as gaining instruction in the Temple by hearing and asking questions: the one is almost useless without the other. We should ask questions of our book and of ourselves; what is its purpose; by what means it proceeds to effect that purpose: whether we fully understand the one, whether we go along with the other. Do the arguments satisfy us, do the descriptions convey lively and distinct images to us; do we understand all the allusions to persons or things? in short does our mind act over again from the writer's guidance what his acted before; do we reason as he reasoned, conceive as he conceived, think and feel as he thought and felt; or if not, can we discern where and how far we do not, and can we tell why we do not?

And now in conclusion, if the mind be thus cultivated and exercised, we stand as it were on the edge of the great garden of knowledge, free to turn on which path we choose, with an instrument of surpassing power to make any portion of it yield its fruits for our nourishment and enjoyment. Happily indeed the choice is fixed for most of us, our calling in life decides for us the particular branch of knowledge, whether physical or moral, which we are most required to study. And inclination or accidental circumstances may farther suggest such branches as we may choose to study besides, in such hours of leisure as we can command. Only it is clear that in whatever it is our duty to act, those matters also it is our duty to study; there are many things of which we must all be ignorant many of which we may be ignorant because there are other studies which we prefer to follow: but there are two things of which, unless we wholly go out of the world, we may not be ignorant without great blame, our duties as men and citizens. And thus the very matters which concern us most nearly, are exactly those on which the rules of this [a Mechanics' Institute] and other similar institutions forbid us to enter. I do not dispute the expediency of these rules, or to speak more correctly, their necessity, in the present state of party feeling, both religious and political: but so long as they are observed, it is idle to call Mechanics' Institutes places of adult education. Physical science alone can never make a man educated; even the formal sciences, invaluable as they are with respect to the discipline of the reasoning powers, cannot instruct the judgement; it is only moral and religious knowledge which can accomplish this. And if habitually removing such knowledge from the course of our studies, we exercise our thoughts and understanding exclusively on lower matters, what will be the result, but that when we come to act upon these higher points, in our relations as citizens and as men, we shall act merely upon ignorance, prejudice, and passion? For notions of moral good and evil of some sort or other we must have; and so also in this country we can hardly help having some notions about political good and evil; but if we take no pains that these notions shall be true and good, what will our lives be but a heap of folly and of sin? This should be borne in mind carefully; and if these merely scientific or literary institutions appear to us to be sufficient for our instruction, if having learnt all that they can teach us, the knowledge so gained shall hide from us our moral ignorance, and make us look upon ourselves as educated men, then they will be more than inefficient, or incomplete; they will have been to us positively mischievous. But if we are well aware of their deficiencies, and take them only at their real value, they may furnish us with some knowledge that may be of use to us in our several callings, and they may undoubtedly give us some innocent and wholesome recreation. They may do more than this, however, if they encourage in us habits of unimpassioned inquiry; if they make us hold commune with our minds, and teach us to feel the difference between understanding a subject and not understanding it. In this manner they may prepare us for the study of those higher matters on which they themselves do not enter; they may make us feel our ignorance where we are ignorant, and the vagueness of our notions where they are vague: they may thus preserve us from presumption on the one hand, and yet, by stimulating the desire of knowledge, may save us from an idolatrous leaning upon human authority on the other; so helping to cherish a state of mind at once docile and inquiring, which best becomes us both as men and as Christians. [*MW*, pp. 420–4.]

Education as only a minor part of much wider social problems

Education is wanted to improve the physical condition of the people, and yet this physical condition must be improved before they can be susceptible to education. [*SL*, LXXXIV, 29 September 1834, p. 338.]

And the hopes entertained by many of the effects to be wrought by new churches and schools, while the social evils of their condition are left uncorrected, appear to me to be utterly wild. [*SL*, ccxiii, 29 December 1839, p. 208.]

In this as in every town, there are opportunities continually arising for establishing societies for some beneficial purpose or other: and they who feel that the whole condition of the poor requires to be improved, will be anxious to encourage, not some of these only, but all. Hitherto our efforts have been too much divided; because our views of the existing evil have been only partial and inadequate. One part of our population has been active in establishing and supporting religious societies; they have been zealous for national and other schools,—for the spreading of religious tracts,—for the encouragement of foreign missions,—and the circulation of the Scriptures; others, again, have highly valued the effects of savings-banks and benefit societies; while others have turned their attention more particularly to the relief of the poor in sickness, whether by hospitals or dispensaries. But, in fact, all these engines should work together, or else the operation of each loses more than half its power. And particularly with regard to the religious improvement of the poor, it is certain that their social degradation is one of the greatest bars to it; and that he can scarcely speak to them with success on spiritual subjects who does not seem to be keenly alive to their worldly evils, and to feel towards them in his actual dealings an unaffected spirit of brotherhood. [*Sermons*, vol. 2, pp. 266–7.]

Property as a vehicle for the education of the people

Most wisely has Mr Laing said in his most instructive account of Norway, that 'a man may read and write and yet have a totally uneducated mind; but that he who possesses property, whether he can read and write or not, has an educated mind; he has forethought, caution, and reflection guiding every action; he knows the value of self-restraint and is in the constant habitual practice of it'. What we commonly call education is invaluable when it is given in time to a people possessing the education of property;—when it opens to them intellectual enjoyments whilst they are yet in a condition to taste them,—and so, by accustoming them to raise their standard of happiness, it prevents them from recklessly sinking to a lower condition. Education, in the common sense of the word, is required by a people before poverty has made havoc amongst them;—at that critical moment when civilisation makes its first burst,—and is accompanied by an immense commercial activity. Then is the time for general education, to teach the man of smaller means how to conduct himself in the coming fever of national development:—to make him understand the misery of sinking from the condition of a proprietor to that of a mere labourer; and if this cannot be avoided at home, then to dispose him to emigrate to a new country, whilst he still retains the habits which will make him a valuable element in a new society there. But can what is called education,—can book learning really educate beggars, or those whose condition is so low that it cannot become lower? Our population want book knowledge, and they also want the means in point of social well-being to render this knowledge available. This is the difficulty of the problem that we know not where to begin. And we shall have gained something, if we are well convinced that no single measure, whether of so called education, or of emigration, or of an improved poor-law,—and far less any political privilege which when given to men unfit to use it is an evil to themselves rather than a good,—will be of real efficacy to better our condition. [*MW*, pp. 480–1.]

The education of the lower class to a new way of life through involvement in management

Undoubtedly it is a matter of public concern that our great towns be not injured at the discretion of every individual speculator, who runs out street after street, and row after row of houses, till the working man in the heart of the town can neither breath fresh air, nor find any open ground within his reach on which he can venture without being guilty of a trespass. It would be no slight benefit, if public walks and gardens, and still more public places of exercise, so laid out as to be ornamental as well as useful and agreeable, were of necessity attached to every great town in the empire. And it might be fairly imperative on every man who builds a certain number of houses, to annex to them a certain portion of ground which might never be built upon, and which should serve in various ways for the sports and recreation of the inhabitants.

I know it is said that the poorer people have no respect for works of art, nor for public property; that if indiscriminately admitted to museums, libraries, churches, or gardens, their greatest pleasure would be to do mischief. True it is, that the poor do not respect these things in England as much as they do abroad; and why? because they have never been thought capable of enjoying them, and therefore have been carefully denied access to them. Certain it is, that they never will respect them, till they are allowed to have an interest in them; but, I should think it well worth while to risk the injury or destruction of a great many works of art, that the people might at last, as they surely would, become fond of these things, and feel that it was indeed a public injury to misuse them. And as a step to this, I have thought that advantage might in the first instance be taken of any societies actually formed amongst the working classes, such as benefit clubs, self-supporting dispensaries, political unions, or the like: and that it would be well worth the while of benevolent individuals to assist in the formation of libraries, or museums, or if possible in renting ground to serve for a public garden and place of amusement, not to be open at first to all the working classes, but to be placed under the management of one or more of these societies for the benefit of their own members. I say 'placed under the management of these societies', perhaps with the addition of one or two honorary members of the richer classes, who might advise without being able to control their poorer associates; for it is most important to put the poor in authority, to intrust them with the care of property, and with the making and enforcing of regulations for its protection and improvement. The true and only way to make civil society really deserving of its name, is to give its members an active and not merely a passive part in the management of its concerns. [*MW*, pp. 215–16.]

'Centralising' the direction of education and fear for the survival of foundations

If ever the question of National Education comes definitely before the Government, I am very desirous of their not 'centralising' too much, but availing themselves of existing machinery which might be done to a great extent, with very little expense, and none of that interference with private institutions, or even with foundations, of which there is so great, and I think in some respects, a reasonable fear. [*SL*, LXXIX, 11 June 1834, p. 333.][2]

CHRISTIAN EDUCATION

Religious and christian education, with some reference to lower-class schools

Now consider what a religious education in the true sense of the word is:—it is no other than a training our children to life eternal; no other than the making them know and love God, know and abhor evil; no other than the fashioning all the parts of our nature for the very ends which God designed for them; the teaching our understandings to know the highest truth, the teaching our affections to love the highest good.

Now can our schools and schoolmasters do this, as surely as they can teach children to read and write? Can they educate as certainly as they can instruct? If they can, then surely they must be the very greatest blessing in the whole world,—their value must be above all counting: to withold them from any of our brethren is to withold from him life eternal; to give them, is not only to open the door of the kingdom of heaven, but actually to lead men into it.

But what God's word itself cannot do surely, cannot be done by any subordinate institution in the Church. Christ appointed His Church to be for the edifying, that is, the improving or causing the growth of the body of Christ, till we all come in the unity of the faith. Has the Church ever, from the beginning, answered fully this glorious end to all its members; has it answered it surely and of necessity? We all but too well know and feel the answer. So neither can schools and schoolmasters surely give religious education to our children, as they can surely teach them to write and read.

And therefore he who thinks that to provide schools is to provide education, or that to provide schools where the Bible and Catechism are taught is to provide religious education, will undoubtedly be disappointed when he sees the fruit of his work. Be sure that the saving men's souls is not such easy matter; our great enemy is not so easily vanquished. It is not the subscription of some pounds or hundreds of pounds, nor the building of a schoolhouse, nor the appointing a schoolmaster, nor the filling the school with all the children in the parish, which will deliver all those children's souls from death, and mortify in them all the lusts of their evil nature, and foster and perfect all the works of the Spirit of God. Schools cannot as a matter of certainty do this, but let us see what they can do.

They can give elementary religious instruction. As every child can be taught to read and write, so every child can be taught to say his Catechism, can be taught to know the main truths of the gospel, can be taught to say hymns. There is no doubt, I suppose, that schools can certainly compass as much as this, and this is, I think, by no means to be despised. For although we know but too well that the learning this and much more than this, is very far from saving our souls certainly or generally, yet it is no less true that without this we are much worse off, and with this much better off. It is at least giving a man a map of the road which he is going, which will keep him in the right way if he uses it. The map will not make his limbs stronger, nor his spirits firmer; he may be tired or he may be indolent, and it is of no use to him then.

I have said that schools can certainly give religious instruction, but that it is not certain that they will give religious education. I dwell on this distinction for two several reasons: first, because it concerns us all in our own private relations, to be aware of the enormous difference between the two; secondly, because, confounding them together, we either expect schools to educate, which very likely they will not be able to do, and then are unreasonably disappointed; or else, feeling sure that the greater good of education is not certainly to be looked for, we do not enough value the lesser good of instruction which can be given certainly, and thus do not encourage schools as much as we ought. The Elementary instruction in religion as in other things, may be certainly given to all who have their common natural faculties; that is, as I said, the Catechism and hymns may be made to be learnt by heart, and the great truths of Christ's Gospel may be taught so as to be known and remembered. But even instruction, when we go beyond the elements of learning, cannot be given to all certainly; we cannot undertake to make every boy, even if we have the whole term of his boyhood and youth given to us for the experiment, either a good divine, or a good scholar, or to be a master of any other kind of knowledge. This cannot be done, although, as far as instruction is concerned, schools have great means at their command, nor do other things out of school very much interfere with their efficacy. But to give a man a Christian education, is to make him love God as well as know him, to make him have faith in Christ, as well as to have been taught the facts that He died for our sins and rose again; to make him open his heart eagerly to every impulse of the Holy Spirit, as well as to have been taught the fact as it is in the Nicene Creed, that He is the Lord and giver of spiritual life. And will mere lessons do all this,—when the course of life and all examples around, both at home and at school, with a far more mighty teaching, and one to which our natural dispositions far more readily answer, enforce the contrary? And therefore the great work of Christian education is not the direct and certain fruit of building schools and engaging schoolmasters, but something far beyond, to be compassed only by the joint efforts of all the whole church and nation,—by the schoolmaster and the parent, by the schoolfellow at school, and by the brothers and sisters at home, by the clergyman in his calling, by the landlord in his calling, by the farmer and the tradesman, by the labourer and the professional man, and the man of independent income, whether large or small, in theirs, by the queen and her ministers, by the great council of the nation in parliament; by each and all of these labouring to remove temptations to evil, to make good easier and more honoured, to confirm faith and holiness in others by their own example; in a word, to make men love and glorify their God and Saviour when they see the blessed fruits of His kingdom even here on earth. And to bring this to ourselves more closely as private persons, let us remember that if we send our children to school, although we give up their instruction to the schoolmaster, yet we cannot give up their education. Their education goes on out of school as well as in school, and very often far more vigorously. We shall see this, if we remember again that the great work of education is to make us love what is good, and therefore not only know it, but do it. And thus we are being educated in a manner always; that is, the people about us and the circumstances about us are constantly producing an effect upon us; they strengthen good in us, or they weaken it; they excite us to love or to dislike something, and according as that thing so loved or so disliked is good or evil, so is our education advanced or hindered. Thus, a parent's example of covetousness, or love of pleasure, or of passionate temper, or of any other fault, is very far more powerful than the schoolmaster's instructions; he uneducates much more than the schoolmaster educates. And thus while we subscribe for schools, we do in fact destroy our own work so far as by any evil or folly of our own we set an evil example instead of a good; encouraging places of religious instruction on the one hand, hindering religious education on the other.

But then will nothing less than such a general co-operation of all classes ensure the great work of Christian education; and we look to schools in themselves as to nothing more than to places of Christian instruction, and not of education? It is most true that without such co-operation, schools, however good in themselves, can never become generally, far less universally, the effective means of Christian education. But let us observe again, that the great good of Christian instruction they will give to all; and we may add, that the far higher blessing of Christian education they will give to many. They will give it to many, and the number will be increased according as the schools become in themselves better and better. A school does its best to educate as well as to instruct, when not only does the teacher's example agree with his teaching, but when he does his endeavour to make the example and influence of the boys themselves—a far greater matter than his own—agree with it also. If he can succeed in this, his school will be to many a place of real Christian education; it will have taught them to know Christ, and helped them to love and obey Him. And though, whilst other influences remain as they are, the example and influence of boys on each other will always be of a mixed character, partly bad as well as partly good; and although therefore a great many will go from school instructed in some degree, but not educated; yet if we multiply schools, and every one sends forth only a few who have really received the blessing of a Christian education, the few so educated by each will be a great many educated by all; and will be by God's blessing a leaven working in the mass of the meal, till, I dare not say the whole of it, but a larger and still a larger part be leavened. [*Sermons*, vol. 5, pp. 88–96.]

Knowledge of poverty, sickness and old age necessary for the completion of a christian education, even at school

In the country, many a young man knows something, at least, of his poorer neighbours; but in towns, the numbers of the poor, and the absence of any special connection between him and any of them in particular, hinder him, too often, from knowing anything of them at all: an evil as much to be regretted on the one side as the other; and which is quite as mischievous to the minds and tempers of the rich as it is to the bodily condition of the poor.

I can imagine hardly anything more useful to a young man of an active and powerful mind, advancing rapidly in knowledge, and with high distinction either actually obtained, or close in prospect, than to take him—or much better, that he should go of himself—to the abodes of poverty and sickness, and old age. Every thing there is a lesson; in every thing Christ speaks, and the Spirit of Christ is ready to convey to his heart all that he witnesses. Accustomed to all the comforts of life, and hardly ever thinking what it would be to want them, he sees poverty and all its evils,—scanty room, and too often scanty fuel, scanty clothing, and scanty food. Instead of the quiet and neatness of his own chamber, he finds, very often, a noise and a confusion which would render deep thought impossible; instead of the stores of knowledge with which his own study is filled, he finds, perhaps, only a prayer-book and a Bible. Nor is this most profitable duty of visiting the poor, as I have said on former occasions, one which you can only practise hereafter, and which does not concern you here. Those who really think of their own souls, and who are desirous of improving them, would find that even here it is by no means impossible. It would indeed be a blessed thing, and would make this place really a seminary of true religion and useful learning, if those among us who are of more thoughtful years, and especially those who are likely to become ministers of Christ hereafter, would remember that their Christian education has commenced already, and that he cannot learn in Christ's school who does not acquaint himself something with the poor. [*Sermons*, vol. 2, pp. 170–2.]

Overt love and admiration of goodness essential, while sceptical doubts should be repressed by the will

I had observed, with some pain, what seemed to me indications of a want of enthusiasm, in the good sense of the word, of a moral sense and feeling corresponding to what I knew was your intellectual activity. I did not observe anything amounting to a sneering spirit; but there seemed to me a coldness on religious matters, which made me fear lest it should change to sneering, as your understanding became more vigorous: for this is the natural fault of the undue predominance of the mere intellect, unaccompanied by a corresponding growth and liveliness of the moral affections, particularly that of admiration and love of moral excellence, just as superstition arises, where it is honest, from the undue predominance of the affections, without the strengthening power of the intellect advancing in proportion. I observed nothing more than an apparent want of lively moral susceptibility. Your answers on religious subjects were always serious and sensible, and seemed to me quite sincere; I only feared that they proceeded, perhaps too exclusively, from an intellectual perception of truth, without a sufficient love and admiration for goodness. [*SL*, LXIV, 15 July 1833, pp. 313–14.]

All speculations of the kind in question [sceptical doubts] are to be repressed by the will, and if they haunt us, notwithstanding the efforts of our will, that then they are to be prayed against, and silently endured as a trial. I mean speculations turning upon things wholly beyond our reach, and where the utmost conceivable result cannot be truth, but additional perplexity. Such must be the question as to the origin and continued existence of moral evil;

which is a question utterly out of our reach, as we know and can know nothing of the system of the universe, and which can never bring us to truth; because if we adopt one hypothesis as certain, and come to a conclusion upon one theory, we shall be met by difficulties quite as insuperable on the other side, which would oblige us in fairness to go over the process again, and to reject our new conclusion, as we had done our old one; because in our total ignorance of the matter, there will always be difficulties in the way of any hypothesis which we cannot answer, and which will effectually preclude our ever arriving at a state of intellectual satisfaction, such as consists in having a clear view of a whole question from first to last, and seeing that the premises are true, the conclusions fairly drawn, and that all objections to either may be satisfactorily answered. This state, which alone I suppose deserves to be called knowledge, is one which, if we can ever attain it, is attainable only in matters merely human, and only within the range of our understanding and experience. Yet if the sight of wickedness in ourselves or others were to lead us to perplex ourselves as to its origin, instead of struggling against it and attempting to put an end to it, we know that we should be wrong, and that evil would thrive and multiply on such a system of conduct.

This would have been the language of a heathen Stoic or Academician, when an Epicurean beset him with the difficulty of accounting for evil without impugning the power or the goodness of the gods. But I think that with us the authority of Christ puts things on a different footing. I know nothing about the origin of evil, but I believe that Christ did know. And I know Christ to have been so wise and so loving to men, that I am sure I may trust His word, and that what was entirely agreeable to His sense of justice and goodness, cannot, unless through my own defect, be otherwise than agreeable to mine. But they (perplexities of the origin of evil kind) should be kept, I think, to ourselves, and not talked of even to our nearest friends, when we once understand their true nature. [*SL*, CII, 21 June 1835, pp. 363–5.]

Christian education not applicable to Unitarians

On inquiring [of your son] to what persuasion his friends belonged, I found that they were Unitarians. I feel that I could not at all enter into the subject [of confirmation], without enforcing principles wholly contrary to those in which your son has been brought up. This difficulty will increase with every half-year that he remains at the school, as he will be gradually coming more and more under my immediate care; and I can neither suffer any of those boys with whom I am more immediately connected, to be left without religious instruction, nor can I give it in his case, without unavoidably imparting views, wholly different from those entertained by the persons he is naturally most disposed to love and honour. Under these circumstances, I think it fair to state to you, what line I shall feel bound to follow, after the knowledge which I have gained of your son's religious belief. I should use every possible pains and delicacy to avoid hurting his feelings with regard to his relations; but at the same time, I cannot avoid labouring to impress on him, what is my belief on the most valuable truths in Christianity, and which, I fear, must be sadly at variance with the tenets in which he has been brought up. In the case of any other form of dissent from the Establishment, I would avoid dwelling on the differences between us, because I could teach all that I conceive to be essential in Christianity, without at all touching upon them. But in this instance, it is impossible to avoid interfering with the very points most at issue. I have a very good opinion of your son, both as to his conduct and abilities, and I should be very sorry to lose him from the school. My difficulty with your son is not one which I feel as a Churchman, but as a Christian; and goes only on this simple principle, that I feel bound to teach the essentials of Christianity to all those committed to my care—and with these the tenets of the Unitarians alone, among all the Dissenters in the kingdom, are in my judgement irreconcileable. [*SL*, VIII, 15 June 1829, pp. 225-6. For attitude to adult Jews and other non-christians, see pp. 161-3.]

THE PROBLEMS OF BOYHOOD

Childhood, boyhood, the inevitable emergence of evil and the responsibility of teachers

For the truth is, that to the knowledge of good and evil we are born, and it must come upon us sooner or later. In the common course of things, it comes about that age with which we are here (Rugby School) most concerned. I do not mean that there are not faults in early childhood—we know that there are;—but we know also that with the strength and rapid growth of boyhood there is a far greater development of these faults, and particularly far less of that submissiveness which belonged naturally to the helplessness of mere childhood. I suppose that, by an extreme care, the period of childhood might be prolonged considerably; but still it must end; and the knowledge of good and evil, in its full force, must come. I believe that this must be; I believe that no care can prevent it, and that an extreme attempt at carefulness, whilst it could not keep off the disorder, would weaken the strength of the constitution to bear it. If we know only evil, it is the condition of hell, and therefore, if schools present an unmixed experience, if there is temptation in abundance, but no support against temptation, and no examples of overcoming it; if some are losing their child's innocence, but none, or very few, are gaining a man's virtue; are we in a wholesome state then? or can we shelter ourselves under the excuse that our evil is unavoidable, that we do but afford, in a mild form, the experience which must be learned sooner or later. It is here that we must be acquitted or condemned. If innocence is exchanged only for vice, then we have not done our part, then the evil is not unavoidable, but our sin: and we may be assured, that for the souls so lost, there will be an account demanded hereafter both of us and you. [*Sermons*, vol. 4, pp. 8–10.]

The transition from childhood to manhood and the need to hasten it

The besetting faults of youth appear to me to arise mainly from its retaining too often the ignorance, selfishness, and thoughtlessness of a child, and having arrived at the same time at a degree of bodily vigour and power, equal, or only a very little inferior, to those of manhood.

And in this state of things, the questions become of exceeding interest, whether the change from childhood to manhood can be hastened, and how far it ought to be hastened. That it ought to be hastened, appears to me to be clear; hastened, I mean, from what it is actually, because in this respect, we do not grow in general fast enough; and the danger of overgrowth is, therefore, small. Besides, where change of one sort is going on very rapidly; where the limbs are growing, and the bones knitting more firmly, where the strength of bodily endurance, as well as of bodily activity, is daily becoming greater; it is self-evident that, if the inward changes which ought to accompany these outward ones are making no progress, there cannot but be derangement and deformity in the system. And, therefore, when I look around, I cannot but wish generally that the change from childhood to manhood in the three great points of wisdom, of unselfishness, and of thoughtfulness, might be hastened from its actual rate of progress in most instances.

But then comes the other great question. 'Can it be hastened, and if it can, how is it to be done?' 'Can it be hastened' means, of course, can it be hastened healthfully and beneficially, consistently with the due development of our nature in its after stages from life temporal to life eternal. For as the child should grow up into the man, so also there is a term of years given in which, according to God's will, the natural man should grow up into the spiritual man; and we must not so press the first change as to make it interfere with the wholesome work of the second. The question then is, really, can the change from childhood to manhood be hastened in the case of boy and young man in general from its actual rate of progress in ordinary cases, without injury to the future excellence and full development of the man? that is, without exhausting prematurely the faculties either of body or mind.

And this is a very grave question, one of the deepest interest for us and for you. For us, as according to the answer to be given to it, should depend our whole conduct and feelings towards you in the matter of your education; for you, inasmuch as it is quite clear, that if the change from childhood to manhood can be hastened safely, it ought to be hastened; and that it is a sin in every one not to try to hasten it; because, to retain the imperfections of childhood when you can get rid of them, is in itself to forfeit the innocence of childhood; to exchange the condition of the innocent infant whom Christ blessed, for that of the unprofitable servant whom Christ condemned. For with the growth of our bodies evil will grow in us unavoidably; and then, if we are not positively good, we are of necessity positively sinners.

Now I believe the only reason that there could be danger in hastening this change [from childhood to manhood] is drawn from the observation of what takes place sometimes with regard to intellectual advancement. It is seen that some young men of great ambition, or remarkable love of knowledge, do really injure their health, and exhaust their minds, by an excess of early study. I always grieve over such cases exceedingly; not only for the individual's sake who is the sufferer, but also for the mischievous effect of his example. It affords a pretence to others to justify their own want of exertion; and those to whom it is in reality the least dangerous, are always the very persons who seem to dread it the most. But we should clearly understand, that this excess of intellectual exertion at an early age, is by no means the same thing with hastening the change from childishness to manliness. We are all enough aware, in common life, that a very clever and forward boy may be, in his conduct, exceedingly childish; that those whose talents and book-knowledge are by no means remarkable, may be, in their conduct, exceedingly manly. Examples of both these truths instantly present themselves to my memory, and perhaps may do so to some of yours. I may say farther, that some whose change from childhood to manhood had been, in St Paul's sense of the terms, the most remarkably advanced, were so far from being distinguished for their cleverness or proficiency in their school-work, that it would almost seem as if their only remaining childishness had been displayed there. What I mean, therefore, by the change from childhood to manhood, is altogether distinct from a premature advance in book-knowledge, and involves in it nothing of that over-study which is dreaded as so injurious.

Yet it is true that I described the change from childhood to manhood, as a change from ignorance to wisdom. I did so, certainly; but yet, rare as knowledge, wisdom is rarer; and knowledge, unhappily, can exist without wisdom, as wisdom can exist with a very inferior degree of knowledge.

Now then, as knowledge of all kinds may be gained without being received, or meant at all to be applied, as the answer to this question, so it may be quite distinct from wisdom. And when I use the term thoughtfulness, as opposed to a child's carelessness, I mean it to express an anxiety for the obtaining of this wisdom. And farther, I do not see how this wisdom, or this thoughtfulness, can be premature in any one; or how it can exhaust before their time any faculties, whether of body or mind. This requires no sitting up late at night, no giving up of

6

healthful exercise; it brings no headaches, no feverishness, no strong excitement at first, to be followed by exhaustion afterwards. Hear how it is described by one who spoke of it from experience. 'The wisdom that is from above is first pure, then peaceable, gentle, easy to be entreated, full of mercy and good fruits, without partiality and without hypocrisy.' There is surely nothing of premature exhaustion connected with any one of these things.

Or, if we turn to the third point of change from childhood to a Christian manhood, the change from selfishness to unselfishness, neither can we find any possible danger in hastening this. This cannot hurt our health or strain our faculties; it can but make life at every age more peaceful and more happy. Nor indeed do I suppose that any one could fancy that such a change was otherwise than wholesome, at the earliest possible period.

There may remain, however, a vague notion, that, generally, if what we mean by an early change from childishness to manliness be that we should become more religious, then, although it may not exhaust the powers, or injure the health, yet it would destroy the natural liveliness and gaiety of youth, and by bringing on a premature seriousness of manner and language, would be unbecoming and ridiculous. Now, in the first place, there is a great deal of confusion and a great deal of folly in the common notions of the gaiety of youth. If gaiety means real happiness of mind, I do not believe that there is more of it in youth than in manhood; for this reason only, that the temper in youth being commonly not yet brought into good order, irritation and passion are felt, probably, oftener than in after life, and these are sad drawbacks, as we all know, to a real cheerfulness of mind. And of the outward gaiety of youth, there is a part also which is like the gaiety of a drunken man; which is riotous, insolent, and annoying to others; which, in short, is a folly and a sin. There remains that which strictly belongs to youth, partly physically—the lighter step and the livelier movement of the growing and vigorous body; partly from circumstances, because a young person's parents and friends stand between him and many of the cares of life, and protect him from feeling them altogether; partly from the abundance of hope which belongs to the beginning of every thing, and which continually hinders the mind from dwelling on past pain. And I know not which of these causes of gaiety would be taken away or lessened by the earlier change from childhood to manhood.

What reason, then, is there for any one's not anticipating the common progress of Christian manliness, and hastening to exchange, as I said before, ignorance for wisdom, selfishness for unselfishness, carelessness for thoughtfulness? I see no reason why we should not; but is there no reason why we should? You are young, and for the most part strong and healthy; I grant that, humanly speaking, the chances of early death to any particular person among you are small. But still, considering what life is, even to the youngest and strongest, it does seem a fearful risk to be living unredeemed; to be living in that state, that if we should happen to die, (it may be very unlikely; but still it is clearly possible,)—that if we should happen to die, we should be most certainly lost for ever. [*Sermons*, vol. 4, pp. 17–30. For similar views see also first part of the next extract.]

The function of public schools to train for responsibility at an early age. The influence at four different age levels of boys on boys for good and evil

I cannot deny that the oldest and most advanced among you have an anxious duty, a duty which some might suppose was too heavy for your years. But it seems to me the nobler as well as the truer way of stating the case to say, that it is the great privilege of this and other such institutions, to anticipate the common term of manhood; that by their whole training they fit the character for manly duties at an age when under another system such duties would be impracticable; that there is not imposed on you too heavy a burden; but that you are capable of bearing without injury what to others might be a burden; and therefore to diminish your duties and lessen your responsibility, would be no kindness, but a degradation; it would be an affront to you, and to the school,—for it would either be saying that you had been incapable of benefiting from the training of a public school system, or that the training, in our particular case, had degenerated; a confession, either way, which God forbid that we should ever be obliged to make, as none could be more disgraceful.

I would say, however, a few words to another class of persons among you, to those whose station in the school is high, but yet does not invest them with actual authority; while their age is often such as to give them really an influence equal to that of those above them, or it may be superior. I will not say that these exercise an influence for evil, for such a charge can only apply to particular persons; none exercise a direct influence for evil without being in some way evil themselves; but I am sure that, as a class, they have much to answer for in standing aloof, and not discouraging evil and encouraging good. They forget that if they have not authority, they have what really amounts to the same thing, they know that they are looked up to,—that what they say and do has its effect on others; they know, in short, that they are of some consequence and weight in the school. But being so, they cannot escape the responsibility of their position. It matters nothing that the rules of the school confer on them no direct power. One far above any school authority has given them a power, and will call them to a strict account for its exercise.

We may lay no official responsibility upon you, but God does. He has given you a talent which it is your sin to waste, or to lay by unimproved. And as it is most certain that you have an influence and power and you well know it; so remember that where there is power, there is ever a duty attached to it;—if you can influence others,—as beyond all doubt you can, and do influence them daily,— if you do not influence them against evil and for good, you are wasting the talent entrusted to you, and sinning against God.

Again, I will speak to those who are yet younger, whose age and station in the school confer on them, it may be, no general influence. But see whether you too have not your influence, and whether you also do not sin often by neglecting it or misusing it. By whom is it that new boys are for the most part corrupted? Not certainly by those much above them in the school, but necessarily by their own immediate companions. By whom they are laughed at for their conscientiousness, or reviled and annoyed for their knowledge or their diligence? Not certainly by those at or near the head of the school, but by those of their own age and form. To whose annoyance does many a new boy owe the wretchedness of his life here? To whose influence and example has he owed the corruption of his practice, and of his principles,—his ruin here and for ever. Is it not to those nearly of his own age, with whom he is most led to associate? And can boys say that they have no influence, when they influence so notoriously the comfort and character of their neighbours? At this moment particularly, when so many new boys are just come amongst us, the younger or middle-aged boys have an especial influence, and let them beware how they use it. I know not what greater sin can be committed, than the so talking, and so acting, to a new boy, as to make him ashamed of any thing good, or not ashamed of any thing evil. It matters very little what is the age of a boy who exercises an influence like this. He too has anticipated the power of more advanced years, and in like manner he has contracted their guilt, and is liable to their punishment.

And now one word for those who are newly come among us, and who form at this moment no very minute portion of our society. If they have brought here good principles and a good practice, let them beware how they suffer them to be lost. They are numerous enough not to be swallowed up at once, as it were, in the society which they have joined; there is some influence which they ought to communicate as well as one which they must receive. The evil which they find may be the most noisy and forward part of our society; let them be satisfied that it does not represent us wholly. Let them be sure that there is much good also amongst us, which would gladly league itself to theirs. Let them not lightly surrender their consciences to a few of the vilest amongst us, as if these few spoke the sentiments and acted the practice of us all. [*Sermons*, vol. 5, pp. 59–63.]

The six evils in school—profligacy, systematic falsehood, cruelty and bullying, active disobedience, idleness, the bond of evil

The actual evil which may exist in a school consists, I suppose, first of all in direct sensual wickedness, such as drunkenness and other things forbidden together with drunkenness in the Scriptures. It would consist, secondly, in the systematic practice of falsehood,—when lies were told constantly by the great majority, and tolerated by all. Thirdly, it would consist in systematic cruelty, or if cruelty be too strong a word, in the systematic annoyance of the weak and simple, so that a boy's life would be miserable unless he learnt some portion of the coarseness and spirit of persecution which he saw all around him.

Fourthly, it would consist in a spirit of active disobedience, —when all authority was hated, and there was a general pleasure in breaking rules simply because they were rules. Fifthly, it would include a general idleness, when every one did as little as he possibly could, and the whole tone of the school went to cry down any attempt on the part of any one boy or more, to shew anything like diligence or a wish to improve himself. Sixthly, there would be a prevailing spirit of combination in evil and of companion-ship; by which a boy would regard himself as more bound to his companions in ties of wickedness, than to God or his neighbour in any ties of good,—so that he would labour to conceal from his parents and from all who might check it, the evil state of things around him; considering it far better that evil should exist, than that his companions doing evil should be punished. And this accomplice spirit, this brotherhood of wickedness, is just the opposite of Christian love or charity; for as St Paul calls charity the bond of perfectness, so this clinging of the evil to one another is the bond of wickedness.

Let these six things exist together, and the profanation of the temple is complete,—it is become a den of thieves. Then whoever passes through such a school may un-doubtedly, by God's grace, be afterwards a good man, but so far as his school years have any effect on his after life, he must be utterly ruined.

The first point which I spoke of was actual profligacy. I cannot dwell upon this, and I truly believe that I need not. Nevertheless, it may be well to consider whether there is not a distinction often between drinking and drunken-ness, which is partly false in itself, and is productive of great mischief. It is partly false in itself, for although it is true that drinking within the bounds of sobriety escapes the sin of drunkenness, and therefore is so far innocent, yet it is no less true that drinking here, whether it be to excess or not, cannot but incur the sin of disobedience, and therefore is so far not innocent but sinful. And the distinction is productive of great mischief; for where many drink, it is quite certain that some will be drunken; it is certain also that many will acquire tastes and habits which lead, if not to actual drunkenness, yet to low and bad society, to idleness and dissipation.

The second point which I spoke of was falsehood. I described the full grown evil as a system where lies were told by the majority and tolerated by all. God forbid that this should be our case; but there is a state of things where lies are told by a few and tolerated by a great many; and if this were laid to our charge, I do not know that I could altogether venture to deny it. I hold it to be the vainest of all vain things to go about to establish by argument the wickedness of a lie. The sense of that wickedness is one of the most elementary feelings of the human mind; if it wants to be persuaded of its reasonableness, it is already corrupted. If a man were to ask for proof that one and one made two, we should scarcely I think, attempt to give it him: we should rather say that his very asking for proof shewed that he was either mad or an idiot. And so it is with the requiring proof of the wickedness of falsehood. In fact, no one does require proof of this: what many want is rather a sense of the great evil of wickedness in itself: they do not say, 'it is not wrong to lie',—but they say, 'there is no great harm in it if it does not injure others'. The mischief is in the expression 'no great harm'; in saying that there is no great harm in any sin; in thinking that sin against God is little in itself except it happen to involve harm to others.

The third point which I noticed was cruelty, or more properly speaking, what is called in schools by a name of its own, 'bullying'. Here, too, I am sure that the picture does not suit our actual state; this evil is one which I am happy to believe is neither general amongst us, nor where it does exist, does it, as I trust and think, exist in any very bad degree. Yet it does exist, undoubtedly, producing, as it ever must, much suffering, and even more evil to the mind of him who is guilty of it. Nothing more surely brutalizes any one, than the allowing himself to find pleasure in the pain or annoyances of others. It degrades and brutalizes too those who stand by and laugh at annoyance so inflicted, instead of regarding it with indignation and disgust.

Fourthly, I spoke of active disobedience; of the pleasure of breaking rules because they were rules; of disliking a thing, in fact, because we like it, or liking it because we dislike it. And here the existence of such a feeling in the heart can only be known by Him who sees the heart. But I can truly say, that regarding the school generally, I have no supicion whatever, I have had no reason ever to suspect, that such a feeling exists amongst you. I do truly believe that from this evil, and a very mischievous evil it is, we are altogether free. I have no apprehension that you regard us as your natural enemies, whose pleasure it is to restrain and annoy you, so that you in your turn should make it your pleasure to disobey and annoy us. Yet such a state of feeling is conceivable in a school, and therefore I thought it right to mention it as one of the evils by which schools might possibly be corrupted.

Fifthly, I spoke of general idleness; of a decided wish prevailing amongst the majority to put down all exertion and all proficiency. I need not say that I do not believe this to be the case here. Nevertheless, we cannot pretend to be wholly free from this evil; it would not be true to say that a diligent boy, desirous of improving himself, never met with any discouragement and even with annoyance. Nay, I must confess, that I have heard before now of instances of this evil which have utterly surprised me, which my own school experience had in no way prepared me to expect. I have heard,—the cases I hope are not common,—but I have heard that boys have been actually ill used by other boys for getting above them, nay, even for shewing a knowledge greater than that of most around them. I could not readily believe that a spirit so utterly paltry and vile would have dared to shew itself at a public school, where mean faults at any rate are mostly discouraged. And truly a meaner or a baser spirit than is betrayed by persecuting or annoying another because he does any thing better than ourselves, or because we wish ourselves to do it ill, and therefore would have no one do it well, is not easily to be met with.

I am come now to the sixth fault, the spirit of combination and companionship. And it were vain to deny that this also exists in some degree amongst us. The feeling of companionship in the bad sense among you, is an unjust and narrow feeling: it is the feeling of one sympathy only, and the being dead to others: it is the feeling of sympathy with one another, which is quite right and good, but it is the absence of sympathy with us, with whom you ought to feel it also, and with your parents, and above all, with Christ, and with God. For when you would fain screen any fault done among you, or would have any evil not put down, one sympathy alone exists among you, and that the very lowest of all. You are alive only to each other's lowest pleasures, are interested for them, and wish to encourage them; but you are dead to each other's highest pleasures, that is, to each other's real good; you are dead to the feeling of sympathy with us, you feel not as we feel, nor as your parents feel, nor as Christ feels. You love not each other strictly speaking, but each other's evil; and you do not love any one else whom you are bound to love, and least of all, God.

This then is the evil of what I call companionship, that

it is by much too narrow. I do not say cease to feel it, for it is good and natural in itself; but I say enlarge it, extend it, carry it on to its full extent; and then what by itself would tend to make us a den of thieves, when enlarged into its full proportions, makes us truly a house of prayer, God's living temple. Let companionship expand into communion. You are companions of one another, with many natural sympathies of age, of employment, of place, and of constitution of body and mind. But you are companions of us too, companions in our common work. [*Sermons*, vol. 5, pp. 66–82.]

The nature of morality and evil

(i) *Low morality of boys and the boyhood of the human race.* From the natural imperfect state of boyhood, they are not susceptible of Christian principles in their full development upon their practice, and I suspect a low standard of morality in many respects must be tolerated amongst them, as it was on a larger scale in what I consider the boyhood of the human race. [*SL*, xxiv, 2 March 1828, p. 75.]

(ii) *The misdemeanours (crimes) of boys are recorded and weighed in the balance.* Let me return to the supposed case of a boy who had incurred a debt, not of a large amount, against the warning of his parents. A boy in such a case would scarcely think that he had done any thing wrong at all, because the sum he would feel was so trifling that it could not inconvenience his friends to pay it. But the act was noted in God's record of the day, and it was noted undoubtedly as a sin; it was noted as a disobedience, it was noted as a want of self-restraint, it was noted as a mark of a want of care over the heart and actions, a want of an abiding faith and dutifulness towards God. It stands as all these in God's record, it stands not as an injury done to a boy's parents, but as an injury to himself; an injury to his good habits of watchfulness, of obedience, of doing all to the glory of God. It stands recorded therefore as a sin, and thus not to be forgotten before God, in whose sight sin never perishes, except so far as it is washed out by Christ's blood.

How many actions, how many words, how many thoughts and feelings of our lives are there which give us no concern at all, and which yet stand recorded as sins before God! It is manifest, then, that the actions of whole days and weeks, passed as they are by too many in utter carelessness, are nothing but one mass of sin; no one thing in them has been sanctified by the thought of God or of Christ. It is no exaggeration, then, but the simple truth, that our sins in such a case are more in number than the hairs of our head; and it might well be the case, that looking at all this vast number, and remembering God's judgement, our hearts, as the Psalmist says of himself, should fail us for fear.

Remember that so many working hours as we have in every day, so many hours have we of sin or of holiness: every hour delivers in and must deliver its record; and every thing so recorded is placed either on one side of the fatal line or on the other; it is charged to our great account of good or of evil. Yes, all that countless multitude of unremembered thoughts, and words and deeds, take their places distinctly, and swell the sum for condemnation or for glory. [*Sermons*, vol. 5, pp. 149–152.]

(iii) *The inheritance and persistence of evil over generations.*[3] If they will colonise with convicts, I am satisfied that the stain should last, not only for one whole life, but for more than one generation; that no convict or convict's child should ever be a free citizen; and that, even in the third generation, the offspring should be excluded from all offices of honour or authority in the colony. This would be complained of as unjust or invidious, but I am sure that distinctions of moral breed are as natural and as just as those of skin or of arbitrary caste are wrong and mischievous; it is a law of God's Providence which we cannot alter, that the sins of the father are really visited upon the child in the corruption of his breed, and in the rendering impossible many of the feelings which are the greatest security to a child against evil. [SL, cxxxvi, 20 July 1836, pp. 415–16.]

THE ROLE, CHARACTER AND DUTIES
OF A HEADMASTER AND STAFF

*The need of undoubted professional status for the teacher and
its natural linkage with the clergy*

As to what regards the position of a schoolmaster in
society, you are well aware that it has not yet obtained that
respect in England, as to be able to stand by itself in
public opinion as a liberal profession; it owes the rank
which it holds to its connection with the profession of a
clergyman, for that is acknowledged universally in England
to be the profession of a gentleman. Mere teaching, like
mere literature, places a man, I think, in rather an equi-
vocal position; he holds no undoubted station in society
by these alone; for neither education nor literature have
ever enjoyed that consideration and general respect in
England, which they enjoy in France and in Germany.
But a far higher consideration is this, that he who is to
educate boys, if he is fully sensible of the importance of
his business, must be unwilling to lose such great opportunities as the clerical character give him, by enabling him
to address them continually from the pulpit, and to admin-
ister the Communion to them as they become old enough
to receive it. [*SL*, cxciv, 19 March 1839, pp. 504–5.]

*The middle-class school teacher; the need for respect, the
need for a link to higher education, the need for a national
organisation*

The schools for the richer classes are, as it is well known,
almost universally conducted by the clergy; and the clergy,
too, have the superintendence of the parochial schools for
the poorer classes. But between these two extremes there
is a great multitude of what are called English, or commercial schools, at which a large proportion of the sons of

farmers and of tradesmen receive their education. In some instances these are foundation schools, and the master is appointed by, and answerable to, the trustees of the charity; but more commonly they are private undertakings, entered upon by individuals as a means of providing for themselves and their families. There is now no restriction upon the exercise of the business of a schoolmaster, and no inquiry made as to his qualifications: the old provision which rendered it unlawful for any man to teach without obtaining a licence from the bishop of the diocese, has naturally and necessarily fallen into disuse; and as the government for the last century has thought it right to leave the moral and religious interests of the people pretty nearly to themselves, an impracticable restriction was suffered to become obsolete, but nothing was done to substitute in its place one that should be at once practicable and beneficial.

Now, in schools conducted by the clergy, the parents have this security, that the man to whom they commit their children has been at least regularly educated, and generally speaking, that he must be a man of decent life. And, if I mistake not, it is merely the prevalence of the feeling that this is so, which has in point of fact given to the clergy nearly the whole education of the richer classes. A man who was not in orders might open a school for the sons of rich parents, if he chose, but he would find it very difficult to get pupils. This state of things has been converted into an accusation against the clergy, by some pretended liberal writers; but it is evidently a most honourable tribute to that union of intellectual and moral qualifications, which, in spite of individual exceptions, still distinguishes the clergy as a body. A layman, who had obtained academical distinctions, would have the same testimony to his intellectual fitness, that a clergyman could boast of, but these distinctions prove nothing as to a man's moral character, whereas, it is felt, and felt justly, that the profession of a clergyman affords to a great extent an evidence of moral fitness also: not certainly as implying any high pitch of positive virtue, but ensuring at least, in common cases, the absence of gross vice; as affording a presumption in short that a man is disposed to be good, and that his faults will be rather those of deficient practice than of habitual carelessness of principle.

But the masters of our English or commercial schools labour under this double disadvantage, that not only their moral but their intellectual fitness must be taken upon trust. I do not mean that this is at all their fault; still less do I say, that they are not fit actually for the discharge of their important duties: but still it is a disadvantage to them that their fitness can only be known after trial,— they have no evidence of it to offer beforehand. They feel this inconvenience themselves, and their pupils feel it also; opportunities for making known their proficiency are wanting alike to both. It has long been the reproach of our law, that it has no efficient *secondary punishments*: it is no less true that we have no regular system of *secondary education.* The classical schools throughout the country have Universities to look to: distinction at school prepares the way for distinction at college; and distinction at college is again the road to distinction and emolument as a teacher: it is a passport with which a young man enters life with advantage, either as a tutor or as a school-master. But any thing like local Universities,—any so much as local distinction or advancement in life held out to encourage exertion at a commercial school, it is as yet vain to look for. Thus the business of education is de-graded: for a schoolmaster of a commercial school having no means of acquiring a general celebrity, is rendered dependent on the inhabitants of his own immediate neighbourhood;—if he offends them, he is ruined. This greatly interferes with the maintenance of discipline; the boys are well aware of their parents' power, and complain to them against the exercise of their master's authority;— nor is it always that the parents themselves can resist the temptation of showing their own importance, and giving the master to understand that he must be careful how he ventures to displease them.

It is manifest that this disadvantage cannot be overcome by the mere efforts of those on whom it presses: the remedy required must be on a larger scale. That the evil occasioned by it is considerable, I can assert with confidence. Submission and diligence are so naturally unwelcome to a boy, that they whose business it is to enforce them have need of a vantage ground to stand upon: they should command the respect of their scholars, not only by their personal qualities, but by their position in society; they should be able to encourage diligence, by pointing out some distinct and desirable reward to which it may attain. For this the interference of Government seems to me indispensible, in order to create a national and systematic course of proceeding, instead of the mere feeble efforts of individuals; to provide for the middling classes something analogous to the advantages afforded to the richer classes by our great public schools and Universities. [*MW*, pp. 227–30.]

The need for a headmaster to have and to express private and controversial views on matters of importance

(1) *In politics.*[4] I conceive that my conduct as to politics can give just offence to the parents of the boys only in one of two ways: that is, either if I were to devote so much time to other matters as to neglect my duty to the school: or if I were in any way to influence the boys' opinions, by letting my own political views appear in my intercourse with my pupils. I feel as strongly as possible

that either of these things be a gross dereliction of duty; but then I feel no way conscious of ever having been guilty of either of them; and with regard to either, I could safely challenge the strictest inquiry. In fact I was so cautious of meddling in any degree with modern politics before the boys, that about eight months ago when we were come in the course of our reading in modern history to the beginning of the first French Revolution, I went back at once to the Middle Ages, because I thought that in spite of the utmost caution it would be impossible to go over the history of very recent events without expressing opinions which in my situation might be supposed likely to influence the boys to my own way of thinking.

What I really have done politically is simply this. I have signed two petitions from Rugby in favour of the Reform Bill, considering it a question of far too great importance for any man to affect to take no part in it. I set up a weekly newspaper in the course of the spring at my own expense, and continued it for about nine weeks; when I was obliged to give it up chiefly from the want of a satisfactory London editor. My object was to circulate it if I could amidst the lower orders; to enlighten them and to improve them. There is nothing in any of my articles there to which I should at all object to put my name,—nothing, as I conceive, at all unbecoming my character as a clergyman, as a gentleman, or as the Master of Rugby School. I hold it to be a most urgent and important duty to every man who has opportunity, to endeavour to furnish something of an antidote to the quantity of wickedness and folly that is circulating through the country. My writing for a newspaper is certainly for no personal interest or gratification whatever; but I hope and believe that what I write may in however humble a degree do some good. [Letter, dated 27 October 1831. These extracts are here produced by kind permission of the Earl of Denbigh.]

(2) *In religion.*[5] I conceive your lordship's question [asking whether Arnold had written the 'Oxford Malignants'] to be one which none but a personal friend has the slightest right to put to me or to any man, I feel it due to myself to decline to give any answer to it. [*SL*, cxxxi, 22 June 1836, p. 411.]

It was because I cannot and do not acknowledge your right officially, as a trustee of Rugby School, to question me on the subject of my real or supposed writings on matters wholly unconnected with the school, that I felt it my duty to decline answering your lordship's question.

It is very painful to be placed in a situation where I must either appear to seek concealment wholly foreign to my wishes, or else must acknowledge a right which I owe it, not only to myself, but to the master of every endowed school in England, absolutely to deny. I have spoken on the subject of the article in the Edinburgh Review freely in the hearing of many, with no request for secrecy on their part expressed or implied. Officially, however, I cannot return an answer—not from the slightest feeling of disrespect to your lordship, but because my answering would allow a principle which I can on no account admit to be just or reasonable. [*SL*, ccxxiii, 27 June 1836, p. 412.]

Unless there is overriding public duty, headmasters ought to avoid scandal as far as possible

I have two principal reasons which make me unwilling to affix my name to my letters in the Herts *Reformer*—one, as I mentioned before, because I am so totally unconnected with the county—which to my feelings is a reason of great weight—my other reason concerns my own particular profession, not so much as a clergyman but as a schoolmaster. I think if I wrote by a name in a newspaper published in another county, I should be thought to be stepping out of the line of my own duties, and courting notoriety as a political writer. And this, I think, I am bound for the school's sake to avoid, unless there is a clear duty on the other side, which I own I cannot as yet perceive to exist. As to the reasons which you urge, of setting an example of moderation in arguing on the question of Church Establishments, it seems to me that the mischief of our newspapers mainly arises from the virulent language which men use while writing anonymously, and that as far as example goes, this is better reproved by temperate writings which are also anonymous. [*SL*, CCXXIII, 14 February 1840, pp. 542–3.]

The necessity of a headmaster being independent of the Governing Body in educational matters

I am only anxious to understand clearly whether he [the head of an educational establishment in Van Diemen's Land] is to be in any degree under the control of any local Board, whether lay or clerical; because, if he were, I could not conscientiously recommend him to undertake an office which I am sure he would shortly find himself obliged to abandon. Uniform experience shows, I think, so clearly the mischief of subjecting schools to the ignorance and party feelings of persons wholly unacquainted with the theory and practice of education, that I feel it absolutely necessary to understand fully the intentions of the Government on this question. [*SL*, CXCVII, 1 July 1839, pp. 506–7.]

The urge to speak out and incur odium grows less with age and the love of a life of ease

I do not like to decline bearing my share of the odium [of stirring up church reform]; thinking that what many men call 'caution' in such matters is too often merely a selfish fear of getting oneself into trouble or ill-will. I am quite sure that I would not gratuitously court odium or controversy, but I must beware also of too much dreading it; and the love of ease, when a man is past five-and-forty, is likely to be a more growing temptation than the love of notoriety, or the pleasure of argument.[6] [*SL*, CCLXIII, 25 January 1841, p. 585.]

The ideal philosophy of school organisation

You know that mine [Rugby School] is a commonwealth, or rather one of Aristotle's or Plato's perfect kingdoms, where the king is superior by nature to all his subjects. My great desire is to teach my boys to govern themselves—a much better thing than to govern them well myself. Only in their case they never can be quite able to govern themselves, and will need some of my government.[7] [*SL*, v, 16 March 1829, p. 221.]

THE ART OF TEACHING

Need to keep the mind active since education is a dynamic process

I am sure that the more active my own mind is, and the more it works upon great moral and political points, the better for the school; not, of course, for the folly of proselytising the boys, but because education is a dynamical, not a mechanical process, and the more powerful and vigorous the mind of the teacher, the more clearly and readily he can grasp things, the better fitted he is to cultivate the mind of another. And to this I find myself coming more and more: I care less and less for information, more and more for the pure exercise of the mind; for answering a question concisely and comprehensively, for showing a command of language, a delicacy of taste, and a comprehensiveness of thought and power of combination. [*SL*, cxix, 2 March 1836, pp. 396–7.]

Need for a teacher to be a student and to love his work

Meantime I write nothing, and read barely enough to keep my mind in the state of a running stream, which I think it ought to be if it would form or feed other minds; for it is ill drinking out of a pond whose stock of water is merely the remains of the long-past rains of the winter and spring, evaporating and diminishing with every successive day of drought. [*SL*, cxi, 12 October 1835, p. 374.]

I hold that a man is only fit to teach so long as he is himself learning daily. If the mind once becomes stagnant, it can give no fresh draught to another mind; it is drinking out of a pond, instead of from a spring. And whatever you read tends generally to your own increase of power, and will be felt by you in a hundred ways hereafter. [*SL*, CXCV, 20 March 1839, p. 506.]

He is the best teacher of others who is best taught himself; that which we know and love we cannot but communicate; that which we know and do not love we soon, I think, cease to know. [*SL*, CCXLII, 17 August 1840, p. 563.]

Need in a teacher for sympathy and liveliness

He who likes boys has probably a daily sympathy with them; and to be in sympathy with the mind you propose to influence is at once indispensable, and will enable you in a great degree to succeed in influencing it.

Another point to which I attach much importance is liveliness. This seems to me an essential condition of sympathy with creatures so lively as boys are naturally, and it is a great matter to make them understand that liveliness is not folly or thoughtlessness. Now I think the prevailing manner amongst many very valuable men at Oxford is the very opposite to liveliness; and I think that this is the case partly with yourself; not at all from affectation, but from natural temper, encouraged perhaps, rather than checked, by a belief that it is right and becoming. But this appears to me to be in point of manner the great difference between a clergyman with a parish and a schoolmaster. It is an illustration of St Paul's rule: 'Rejoice with them that rejoice, and weep with them that weep.' A clergyman's intercourse is very much with the sick and the poor, where liveliness would be greatly misplaced; but a schoolmaster's is with the young, the strong, and the happy, and he cannot get on with them unless in animal spirits he can sympathize with them, and show them that his thoughtfulness is not connected with selfishness and weakness. At least, this applies, I think, to a young man;

for when a teacher gets to an advanced age, gravity, I suppose, would not misbecome him, for liveliness might then seem unnatural, and his sympathy with the boys must be limited, I suppose, then, to their great interests rather than their feelings. [*SL*, ccx, 21 November 1839, pp. 524–5.]

Experience of mountains necessary for education and relaxation

I find Westmoreland very convenient in giving me an opportunity of having some of the Sixth Form with me in the holidays; not to read, of course, but to refresh their health when they get knocked up by the work, and to show them mountains and dales; a great point in education, and a great desideratum to those who only know the central or southern counties of England. [*SL*, lxxx, 25 June 1834, p. 334.]

Need for a complete rest from school affairs in holidays and the need to have 'diversions' while at school

I have had a very troublesome correspondence about school matters, which has brought Rugby more before my mind than I wish to have it in the holidays. I hope that this is not indolence, but I feel it very desirable, if I can, to get my mind thoroughly refreshed and diverted during the vacations—'diverted', I mean in the etymological rather than in the popular sense, that is, turned aside from its habitual objects of interest to others which refresh from their very variety. Thus my History is a great *diversion* from the cares about the school, and then the school work in its turn is a *diversion* from the thoughts about the History. Otherwise either would be rather overpowering, for the History, though very interesting, is a considerable engrosser of one's thoughts; there is so much difficulty in the composition of it, as well as in the investigation of the facts.[8] [*SL*, cclxiii, 25 January 1841, p. 584.]

Duty to purify the school by expulsion and the need for co-operation between public schools, particularly with reference to expulsion

Till a man learns that the first, second, and third duty of a schoolmaster is to get rid of unpromising subjects, a great public school will never be what it might be, and what it ought to be. [Quoted in Stanley, undated, p. 110.]

Sending away boys is a necessary and regular part of a good system, not as a punishment to one, but as a protection to others. Undoubtedly it would be a better system if there was no evil; but evil being unavoidable we are not a jail to keep it in, but a place of education where we must cast it out, to prevent its taint from spreading. [Quoted in Stanley, undated, p. 113.]

It seems to me that we have not enough of co-operation in our system of public education, including both the great schools and Universities. I do not like the centralising plan of compulsory uniformity under the government; but I do not see why we should all be acting without the least reference to one another. Something of this kind is wanted, particularly I think with regard to expulsion. Under actual circumstances it is often no penalty at all in reality, while it is considered ignorantly to be the excess of severity and the ruin of a boy's prospects. [*SL*, xci, 28 January 1835, p. 347.]

EDUCATION IN SCHOOL

Classical education

A reader unacquainted with the real nature of a classical education, will be in danger of undervaluing it, when he sees that so large a portion of time at so important a period of human life is devoted to the study of a few ancient writers, whose works seem to have no direct bearing on the studies and duties of our own generation. For instance, although some provision is undoubtedly made at Rugby for acquiring a knowledge of modern history, yet the History of Greece and Rome is more studied than that of France and England; and Homer and Virgil are certainly much more attended to than Shakespeare and Milton. This appears to many persons a great absurdity; while others who are so far swayed by authority as to believe the system to be right, are yet unable to understand how it can be so. When Latin and Greek were almost the only written languages of civilised man, it is manifest that they must have furnished the subjects of all liberal education. The question therefore is wholly changed, since the growth of a complete literature in other languages; since France, and Italy, and Germany, and England, have each produced their philosophers, their poets, and their historians, worthy to be placed on the same level with those of Greece and Rome.

But although there is not the *same* reason now which existed three or four centuries ago for the study of Greek and Roman literature, yet there is another no less substantial. Expel Greek and Latin from your schools, and you confine the views of the existing generation to themselves and their immediate predecessors: you will cut off so many centuries of the world's experience, and place us in the same state as if the human race had first come into existence in the year 1500. For it is nothing to say that a few learned individuals might still study classical literature; the effect produced on the public mind would be no greater than that which has resulted from the labours of our oriental scholars; it would not spread beyond themselves, and men in general after a few generations would know as little of Greece and Rome, as they do actually of China and Hindostan. But such an ignorance would be incalculably more to be regretted. With the Asiatic mind, we have no nearer connection or sympathy than that which is derived from our common humanity. But the mind of the Greek and of the Roman is in all the essential points of its constitution our own; and not only so, but it is our own mind developed to an extraordinary degree of perfection. Wide as is the difference between us with respect to those physical instruments which minister to our uses or our pleasures, although the Greeks and Romans had no steam-engines, no printing-presses, no mariner's compass, no telescopes, no microscopes, no gunpowder; yet in our moral and political views, in those matters which most determine human character, there is a perfect resemblance in these respects. Aristotle, and Plato, and Thucydides, and Cicero, and Tacitus, are most untruly called ancient writers; they are virtually our own countrymen and contemporaries, but have the advantage which is enjoyed by intelligent travellers, that their observation has been exercised in a field out of the reach of common men; and that having thus seen in a manner with our eyes what we cannot see for ourselves, their conclusions are such as bear upon our own circumstances, while their information has all the charm of novelty, and all the value of a mass of new and pertinent facts, illustrative of the great science of the nature of civilized man.

Now when it is said, that men in manhood so often

throw their Greek and Latin aside, and that this very fact shows the uselessness of their early studies, it is much more true to say that it shows how completely the literature of Greece and Rome would be forgotten, if our system of education did not keep up the knowledge of it. But it by no means shows that system to be useless, unless it followed that when a man laid aside his Greek and Latin books, he forgot also all that he had ever gained from them. This, however, is so far from being the case, that even where the results of a classical education are least tangible, and least appreciated even by the individual himself, still the mind often retains much of the effect of its early studies in the general liberality of its tastes and comparative comprehensiveness of its views and notions.

All this supposes, indeed, that classical instruction should be sensibly conducted; it requires that a classical teacher should be fully acquainted with modern history and modern literature, no less than with those of Greece and Rome. What is, or perhaps what used to be, called a mere scholar, cannot possibly communicate to his pupils the main advantages of a classical education. The knowledge of the past is valuable, because without it our knowledge of the present and of the future must be scanty; but if the knowledge of the past be confined wholly to itself, if, instead of being made to bear upon things around us, it be totally isolated from them, and so disguised by vagueness and misapprehension as to appear incapable of illustrating them, then indeed it becomes little better than laborious trifling, and they who declaim against it may be fully forgiven.

To select one instance of this perversion, what can be more absurd than the practice of what is called construing Greek and Latin, continued as it often is even with pupils of an advanced age? The study of Greek and Latin, considered as mere languages, is of importance, mainly as it enables us to understand and employ well that language in which we commonly think, and speak, and write. It does this because Greek and Latin are specimens of language at once highly perfect and incapable of being understood without long and minute attention: the study of them, therefore, naturally involves that of the general principles of grammar; while their peculiar excellences illustrate the points which render language clear, and forcible, and beautiful. But our *application* of this general knowledge must naturally be to our own language; to show us what are its peculiarities, what its beauties, what its defects; to teach us by the patterns or the analogies offered by other languages, how the effect which we admire in them may be produced with a somewhat different instrument. Every lesson in Greek or Latin may and ought to be made a lesson in English; the translation of every sentence in Demosthenes or Tacitus is properly an exercise in extemporaneous English composition; a problem, how to express with equal brevity, clearness, and force, in our own language, the thought which the original author has so admirably expressed in his. But the system of construing, far from assisting, is positively injurious to our knowledge and use of English; it accustoms us to a tame and involved arrangement of our words, and to the substitution of foreign idioms in the place of such as are national; it obliges us to caricature every sentence that we render, by turning what is, in its original dress, beautiful and natural, into something which is neither Greek nor English, stiff, obscure, and flat, exemplifying all the faults incident to language, and excluding every excellence.

The exercise of translation, on the other hand, meaning, by translation, the expressing of *an entire sentence* of a foreign language by an entire sentence of our own, as opposed to the rendering separately into English either every separate word, or at most only *parts of the sentence*, whether larger or smaller, the exercise of translation is capable of furnishing improvement to students of every age, according to the measure of their abilities and knowledge. The late Dr Gabell, than whom in these matters there can be no higher authority, when he was the under master of Winchester College, never allowed even the lowest forms to *construe*; they always were taught, according to his expression, to *read into English*. From this habit even the youngest boys derived several advantages; the meaning of the sentence was more clearly seen when it was read all at once in English, than when every clause or word of English was interrupted by the intermixture of patches of Latin; and any absurdity in the translation was more apparent. Again, there was the habit gained of constructing English sentences upon any given subject, readily and correctly. Thirdly, with respect to Latin itself, the practice was highly useful. By being accustomed to translate idiomatically, a boy, when turning his own thoughts into Latin, was enabled to render his own natural English into the appropriate expressions in Latin. Having been always accustomed, for instance, to translate 'quum venisset' by the participle 'having come', he naturally, when he wishes to translate 'having come' into Latin, remembers what expression in Latin is equivalent to it. Whereas, if he has been taught to construe literally 'when he had come', he never has occasion to use the English participle in his translations from Latin; and when, in his own Latin compositions, he wishes to express it, he is at a loss how to do it, and not unfrequently, from the construing notion that a participle notion in one language must be a participle in another, renders it by the Latin participle passive; a fault which all who have had any experience in boys' compositions must have frequently noticed.

But as a boy advances in scholarship, he ascends from the idiomatic translation of particular expressions to a similar rendering of an entire sentence. He may be taught that the order of the words in the original is to be preserved as nearly as possible in the translation; and the problem is how to effect this without violating the idiom of his own language. There are simple sentences, such as 'Ardeam Rutuli habebant', in which nothing more is required than to change the Latin accusative into the English nominative, and the active verb into one passive or neuter: 'Ardea belonged to the Rutulians.' And in the same way the other objective cases, the genitive and the dative, when they occur at the beginning of a sentence, may be often translated by the nominative in English, making a corresponding change in the voice of the verb following. But in many instances also the nominative expresses so completely the principle subject of the sentence, that it is unnatural to put it into any other case than the nominative in the translation.

Another point may be mentioned, in which the translation of the Greek and Roman writers is most useful in improving a boy's knowledge of his own language. In the choice of his words, and in the style of his sentences, he should be taught to follow the analogy required by the age and character of the writer whom he is translating. For instance, in translating Homer, hardly any words should be employed except Saxon, and the oldest and simplest of those which are of French origin; and the language should consist of a series of simple propositions, connected with one another only by the most inartificial conjunctions. In translating the tragedians, the words should be principally Saxon, but mixed with many of French or foreign origin, like the language of Shakespeare, and the other dramatists of the reigns of Elizabeth and James I. The term 'words of French origin' is used purposely, to denote that large portion of our language which, although of Latin derivation, came to us immediately from the French of our

Norman conquerors, and thus became a part of the natural
spoken language of that mixed people, which grew out of
the melting of the Saxon and Norman races into one
another. But these are carefully to be distinguished from
another class of words equally of Latin derivation, but
which have been introduced by learned men at a much
later period, directly from Latin books, and have never,
properly speaking, formed any part of the genuine national
language. These truly foreign words, which Johnson used
so largely, are carefully to be shunned in the translation
of poetry, as being unnatural, and associated only with the
most unpoetical period of our literature, the middle of the
eighteenth century.

So also, in translating the prose writers of Greece and
Rome, Herodotus should be rendered in the style and
language of the chroniclers; Thucydides in that of Bacon
or Hooker, while Demosthenes, Cicero, Caesar and
Tacitus, require a style completely modern—the perfection of the English language such as we now speak and
write it, varied only to suit the individual differences of
the different writers, but in its range of words, and in its
idioms, substantially the same.

Thus much has been said on the subject of translation,
because the practice of construing has naturally tended to
bring the exercise into disrepute: and in the contests for
academical honours at both Universities, less and less
importance, we have heard, is constantly being attached
to the power of vivâ voce translation. We do not wonder at
any contempt that is shown towards *construing*, the practice being a mere folly; but it is of some consequence that
the value of *translating* should be better understood, and
the exercise more carefully attended to. It is a mere
chimera to suppose, as many do, that what they call free
translation is a convenient cover for inaccurate scholarship.
It can only be so through the incompetence or carelessness

of the teacher. If the force of every part of the sentence be not fully given, the translation is so far faulty; but idiomatic translation, much more than literal, is an evidence that the translator does see the force of his original; and it should be remembered that the very object of so translating is to preserve the spirit of an author, where it would be lost or weakened by translating literally; but where a literal translation happens to be faithful to the spirit, there of course it should be adopted; and any omission or misrepresentation of any part of the meaning of the original does not preserve its spirit, but, as far as it goes, sacrifices it, and is not to be called 'free translation', but rather 'imperfect', 'blundering', or, in a word, 'bad translation'.

An undue importance is attached by some persons to [modern history as given at Rugby] and those who would care little to have their sons familiar with the history of the Peloponnesian war are delighted that they should study the Campaigns of Frederic the Great or of Napoleon. Information about modern events is more useful, they think, than that which relates to antiquity; and such information they wish to be given to their children.

This favourite notion of filling boys with useful information is likely, we think, to be productive of some mischief. It is a caricature of the principles of inductive philosophy, which, while it taught the importance of a knowledge of facts, never imagined that this knowledge was of itself equivalent to wisdom. Now it is not so much our object to give boys 'useful information', as to facilitate their gaining it hereafter for themselves, and to enable them to turn it to account when gained. [A considerable extract has been omitted here, dealing largely with the purpose of teaching history.]

The fault of systems of classical education in some instances has been, not that they did not teach modern history, but that they did not prepare and dispose their pupils to acquaint themselves with it afterwards; not that they did not attempt to raise an impossible superstructure, but that they did not prepare the ground for the foundation, and put the materials within reach of the builder.

That impatience, which is one of the diseases of the age, is in great danger of possessing the public mind on the subject of education; an unhealthy restlessness may succeed to lethargy. Men are not contented with sowing the seed unless they can also reap the fruit; forgetting how often it is the law of our condition, that 'one soweth and another reapeth'. It is no wisdom to make boys prodigies of information; but it is our wisdom and our duty to cultivate their faculties each in its season, first the memory and imagination, and then the judgement; to furnish them with the means, and to excite the desire, of improving themselves, and to wait with confidence for God's blessing on the result. [*QJEd*, vol. VII, No. XIV, 1834, pp. 239–46, 249. Also reproduced in *MW*.]

Need to enliven the classics

Shakespeare, with English boys, would be but a poor substitute for Homer; but I confess that I should be glad to get Dante and Goethe now and then in the room of some of the Greek tragedians and of Horace; or rather not in their room, but mixed up along with them. [*SL*, CXXXVIII, 23 September 1836, p. 418.]

Rhetoric in sixth form and university

We have been reading some of the Rhetoric in the Sixth Form this half-year, and its immense value struck me again so forcibly, that I could not consent to send my son to a University where he would lose it altogether, and where his whole studies would be formal merely and not real, either mathematics or philology, with nothing at all like the Aristotle and Thucydides at Oxford. In times past, the neglect of philology at Oxford was so shameful, that it almost neutralised the other advantages of the place, but I do not think that this is so now; and the utter neglect of vivâ voce translation at Cambridge is another great evil; even though by construing instead of translating they almost undo the good of their vivâ voce system at Oxford. [*SL*, CCLXXI, 26 June 1841, pp. 598–9.]

The importance and beauty of mathematics; the need to break ground into several of the mines of knowledge (including physical science) when young

You should, without fail, instruct your pupils in the six books of Euclid at least. I am, as you well know, no mathematician, and therefore my judgement in this matter is worth so much the more, because what I can do in mathematics, anybody can do; and as I can teach the first six books of Euclid, so I am sure can you. Then it is a grievous pity that at your age, and with no greater amount of work than you now have, you should make up your mind to be shut out from one great department, I might almost say, from many great departments of human knowledge. Even now I would not allow myself to say that I should never go on in mathematics, unlikely as it is at my age; yet I always think that if I were to go on a long voyage, or were in any way hindered from using many books, I should turn very eagerly to geometry, and other such studies. But further, I do really think that with boys and young men, it is not right to leave them in ignorance of the beginnings of physical science. It is so hard to begin anything in after life, and so comparatively easy to continue what has been begun, that I think we are bound to break ground, as it were, into several of the mines of knowledge with our pupils, that the first difficulties may be overcome by them while there is yet a power from without to aid their own faltering resolution, and that so they may be enabled, if they will, to go on with the study hereafter. I do not think that you do a pupil full justice, if you so entirely despise Plato's authority, as to count geometry in education to be absolutely good for nothing. I am sure that you will forgive me for urging this, for I think it concerns you much, and I am quite sure that you ought not to run the risk of losing a pupil because you will not master the six books of Euclid, which, after all, are not to be despised for one's own very solace and delight; for I do not know that Pythagoras did anything strange, if he sacrificed a hecatomb when he discovered that marvellous relation between the squares containing and subtending a right angle, which the 47th proposition of the first book demonstrates.[9] [SL, ccxxxvii, 8 May 1840, p. 556.]

Evaluation of physical science

If one might wish for impossibilities, I might then wish that my children might be well versed in physical science, but in due subordination to the fulness and freshness of their knowledge on moral subjects. This, however, I believe cannot be; and physical science, if studied at all, seems too great to be studied ἐν παρέργῳ: wherefore, rather than have it the principal thing in my son's mind, I would gladly have him think that the sun went round the earth, and that the stars were so many spangles set in the bright blue firmament. Surely the one thing needful for a Christian and an Englishman to study is Christian and moral and political philosophy. [SL, cxxviii, 9 May 1836, pp. 405–6.]

The study of physical science must be tempered with morals even at the university

I think, too, that physical science can nowhere be so well studied as at Oxford, because the whole spirit of the place is against its undue ascendency; for instance, Anatomy, which in London is dangerously, as I think, made one of the qualifications for a degree, might be, I imagine, profitably required at Oxford, where you need not dread the low morals and manners of so many of the common medical students. [*SL*, CLXXXIV, 5 August 1838(?), p. 483 (B).]

The study of history[10]

History is to be studied as a whole, and according to its philosophical divisions, not such as are merely geographical and chronological; the history of Greece and of Rome is not an idle inquiry about remote ages and forgotten institutions, but a living picture of things present, fitted not so much for the curiosity of the scholar, as for the instruction of the statesman and the citizen. [*MW*, p. 399.]

EXAMINATIONS

Increasing competition in life will inevitably produce an increasing stress on examinations with corresponding dangers to the essence of education

What was accounted great learning some years ago, is no longer reckoned such; what was in the days of our fathers only an ordinary and excusable ignorance, is esteemed as something disgraceful now. In these things, as in all others, never was competition so active,—never were such great exertions needed to obtain success. Those who are in the world know this already; and if there are any of you who do not know it, it is fit that you should be made aware of it. Every profession, every institution in the country, will be strung up to a higher tone: examinations will be more common and more searching: the qualifications for every public and profitable or honourable office, will be raised more and more. All this *will* be certainly, and no human power can stop it: and I think also, that it ought to be. Undoubtedly knowledge is good, and in the general improvement of our faculties I know not where we ought to desire to stop. I know not that our bodies can be too strong and active:—I know not that our knowledge can be too extensive, or our perception of truth too clear. But 'everything in its own order'. While pursuing so hard a course of study—while apt to be so engrossed with these exercises of the intellect,—while the leaves of the tree are growing out into such beautiful luxuriance,—what is to become of the fruit? What is to become of that part of us which is fitted for more than earthly happiness? There are two parts of our nature, which are in a manner the very seed of eternal life:—our feelings of humility and love. What will become of us if the strong and intense pursuit after intellectual excellence smother these? [*Sermons*, vol. 2, pp. 166–7.]

The value of viva voce examinations at school and university

I found by the reports, which I received this morning, that a resolution had been passed that the examinations [of London University] should be conducted entirely through the medium of printed papers. I think that this is a point on which the experience of Oxford, entirely confirmed in my judgement by my own experience here, is well deserving of consideration,—because we habitually use and know the value of printed papers, and we know also the advantages to be derived from a vivâ voce examination, of which Cambridge has made no trial. I think that these advantages are much too great to be relinquished by us altogether.

1st. The exercise of extempore translation is the only thing in our system of education which enables a young man to express himself fluently and in good language without premeditation. Wherever it is attended to, it is an exercise of exceeding value; it is, in fact, one of the best possible modes of instruction in English composition, because the constant comparison with the different idioms of the languages, from which you are translating, shows you in the most lively manner the peculiar excellences and defects of our own; and if men are tried by written papers only, one great and most valuable talent, that of readiness, and the very useful habit of retaining presence of mind, so as to be able to avail oneself without nervousness of all one's knowledge, and to express it at once by word of mouth, are never tried at all.

2nd. Nothing can equal a vivâ voce examination for trying a candidate's knowledge in the contents of a long history or of a philosophical treatise. I have known men examined for two hours together vivâ voce in Aristotle, and they have been thus tried more completely than could be done by printed papers; for a man's answers suggest continually further questions; you can at once probe his weak points; and, where you find him strong, you can give him an opportunity of doing himself justice, by bringing him out especially on those very points.

3rd. Time is saved, and thereby weariness and exhaustion of mind to both parties. A man can speak faster than he can write, and he is relieved by the variety of the exercise.

4th. The éclat of vivâ voce examination is not to be despised. When a clever man goes into the schools at Oxford, the room is filled with hearers of all ranks in the University. His powers are not merely taken on trust from the report of the examiners; they are witnessed by the University at large, and their peculiar character is seen and appreciated also. I have known the eloquence of a man's translations from the poets and orators and historians, and the clearness and neatness of his answers in his philosophical examination, long and generally remembered, with a distinctiveness of impression very different from that produced by the mere knowledge that he is in the

first class. And in London, the advantages of such a public
vivâ voce examination would be greater of course than
anywhere else, because the audience might be larger and
more mixed.

5th. Presence of mind is a quality which deserves to be
encouraged—nervousness is a defect which men feel
painfully in many instances through life. Education should
surely attach some reward to a valuable quality which may
be acquired in great measure by early practice, and should
impose some penalty or some loss on the want of it. Now,
if you have printed papers, you effectually save a man from
suffering too much from his nervousness; but if you have
printed papers *only*, you do not, I think, encourage as you
should do the excellence of presence of mind, and the
power of making our knowledge available on the instant.

6th. It is an error to suppose that no exact judgement of
a man can be formed from a vivâ voce examination. Like
all other things, such an examination requires some attention and some practice on the part of those who conduct it;
but all who have had much experience in it are well aware
that, combined with an examination on paper, it is entirely
satisfactory. In fact, either system, of papers, or of vivâ
voce examination, if practised exclusively, does not half
try the men. Each calls forth faculties which the other
does not reach equally. [*SL*, CLXXVIII, 17 March 1838,
pp. 475–7.]

Organised examinations necessary for the education of girls

I feel quite as strongly as you do the extreme difficulty of
giving to girls what really deserves the name of education
intellectually. But there is nothing for girls like the Degree
Examination, which concentrates one's reading so beautifully, and makes one master a certain number of books
perfectly. And unless we had a domestic examination for
young ladies to be passed before they came out, and

another like the great go, before they come of age, I do
not see how the thing can ever be effected. Seriously, I do
not see how we can supply sufficient encouragement for
systematic and laborious reading, or how we can ensure
many things being retained at once fully in the mind,
when we are wholly without the machinery which we have
for our boys. [*SL*, CCLVIII, 2 January 1841, pp. 580–1.]

BOYS—DISCIPLINE, IDLENESS, READING, ETC.

Flogging and fagging

The points which are attacked in [the system of discipline
in our schools] are two—flogging and fagging; and we will
first consider the question of flogging. We have nothing to
do with arguments against the excessive or indiscriminate
use of such a punishment: it is but idle to attack what no
one defends, and what has at present hardly any real
existence. The notion of a schoolmaster being a cruel
tyrant, ruling only by the terror of the rod, is about as real
as the no less terrific image of Bluebeard. The fault of the
old system of flogging at Winchester was not its cruelty,
but its inefficiency; the punishment was so frequent and
so slight as to inspire very little either of terror or of
shame. In other schools, eighty or a hundred years ago,
there may have been a system of cruel severity, but
scarcely, I should imagine, within the memory of anyone
now alive. But the argument against *all* corporal punishment applies undoubtedly to an existing state of things;
and this argument, therefore, I shall proceed to consider.

'Corporal punishment,' it is said, 'is degrading.' I well
know of what feeling this is the expression; it originates
in that proud notion of personal independence which is
neither reasonable nor Christian, but essentially barbarian.
It visited Europe in former times with all the curses of
the age of chivalry, and is threatening us now with those

of Jacobinism. For so it is, that the evils of ultra-aristoc-
racy and ultra-popular principles spring precisely from the
same source—namely, from selfish pride—from an idolatry
of personal honour and dignity in the aristocratical form
of the disease—of personal independence in its modern
and popular form. It is simply impatience of inferiority
and submission—a feeling which must be more frequently
wrong or right, in proportion to the relative situation and
worthiness of him who entertains it, but which cannot be
always or generally right except in beings infinitely more
perfect than man. Impatience of inferiority felt by a child
towards his parents, or by a pupil towards his instructors, is merely wrong, because it is at variance with
the truth: there exists a real inferiority in the relation,
and it is an error, a fault, a corruption of nature, not to
acknowledge it.

Punishment, then, inflicted by a parent or a master for
the purposes of correction, is in no true sense of the word
degrading; nor is it the more degrading for being corporal.
To say that corporal punishment is an appeal to personal
fear is a mere abuse of terms. In this sense all bodily pain
or inconvenience is an appeal to personal fear; and a man
should be ashamed to take any pains to avoid the tooth-
ache or the gout. Pain is an evil; and the fear of pain, like
all other natural feelings, is of mixed character, sometimes
useful and becoming, sometimes wrong and mischievous.
I believe that we should not do well to extirpate any of
these feelings, but to regulate and check them by cherish-
ing and strengthening such as are purely good. To destroy
the fear of pain altogether, even if practicable, would be
but a doubtful good, until the better elements of our nature
were so perfected as wholly to supersede its use. Perfect
love of good is the only thing which can profitably cast
out all fear. In the meanwhile, what is the course of true
wisdom? Not to make a boy insensible to bodily pain, but

to make him dread moral evil more; so that fear will do its proper and appointed work, without so going beyond it as to become cowardice. It is cowardice to fear pain or danger more than neglect of duty, or than the commission of evil; but it is useful to fear them, when they are but the accompaniments or the consequences of folly and of faults.

It is very true that the fear of punishment generally (for surely it makes no difference whether it be the fear of the personal pain of flogging, or of the personal inconvenience of what have been proposed as its substitutes, confinement, and a reduced allowance of food,) is not the highest motive of action; and therefore, the course actually followed in education is most agreeable to nature and reason, that the fear of punishment should be appealed to less and less as the moral principle becomes stronger with advancing age. If any one really supposes that young men in the higher forms of public schools are governed by fear, and not by moral motives; that the appeal is not habitually made to the highest and noblest principles and feelings of their nature, he is too little aware of the actual state of those institutions to be properly qualified to speak or write about them.

With regard to the highest forms, indeed, it is well known that corporal punishment is as totally out of the question in the practice of our schools as it is at the universities; and I believe that there could nowhere be found a set of young men amongst whom punishment of any kind was less frequent, or by whom it was less required. The real point to be considered is merely, whether corporal punishment is in all cases unfit to be inflicted on boys under fifteen, or on those who, being older in years, are not proportionably advanced in understanding or in character, who must be ranked in the lower part of the school, and who are little alive to the feeling of self-respect, and little capable of being influenced by moral motives. Now, with regard to young boys, it appears to me positively mischievous to accustom them to consider themselves insulted or degraded by personal correction. The fruits of such a system were well shown in an incident which occurred in Paris during the three days of the revolution of 1830. A boy of twelve years old, who had been forward in insulting the soldiers, was noticed by one of the officers; and though the action was then raging, the officer, considering the age of the boy, merely struck him with the flat part of his sword, as the fit chastisement for boyish impertinence. But the boy had been taught to consider his person sacred, and that a blow was a deadly insult; he therefore followed the officer, and having watched his opportunity, took deliberate aim at him with a pistol, and murdered him. This was the true spirit of the savage, exactly like that of Callum Beg in Waverley, who, when a 'decent gentleman' was going to chastise him with his cane for throwing a quoit at his shins, instantly drew a pistol to vindicate the dignity of his shoulder. We laugh at such a trait in the work of the great novelist, because, according to our notions, the absurdity of Callum Beg's resentment is even more striking than its atrocity. But I doubt whether to the French readers of Waverley it has appeared either laughable or disgusting; at least the similar action of the real Callum in the streets of Paris was noticed at the time as something entitled to our admiration. And yet what can be more mischievous than thus to anticipate in boyhood those feelings which even in manhood are of a most questionable nature, but which, at an earlier period, are wholly and clearly evil? At an age when it is almost impossible to find a true, manly sense of the degradation of guilt or faults, where is the wisdom of encouraging a fantastic sense of the degradation of personal correction? What can be more false, or more adverse to the simplicity, sobriety, and humbleness of mind which are the best ornament of youth, and offer the best promise of a noble manhood? There is an essential inferiority in a boy as compared with a man, which makes an assumption of equality on his part at once ridiculous and wrong; and where there is no equality, the exercise of superiority implied in personal chastisement cannot in itself be an insult or a degradation.

The total abandonment, then, of corporal punishment for the faults of young boys appears to me not only uncalled for, but absolutely to be deprecated. It is of course most desirable that all punishment should be superseded by the force of moral motives; and up to a certain point this is practicable. All endeavours so to dispense with flogging are the wisdom and the duty of a schoolmaster; and by these means the amount of corporal punishment inflicted may be, and in fact has been, in more than one instance, reduced to something very inconsiderable. But it is one thing to get rid of punishment by lessening the amount of faults, and another to say, that even if the faults are committed, the punishment ought not to be inflicted. Now it is folly to expect that faults will never occur; and it is very essential towards impressing on a boy's mind the natural imperfectness and subordination of his condition, that his faults and the state of his character being different from what they are in after life, so the nature of his punishment should be different also, lest by any means he should unite the pride and self-importance of manhood with a boy's moral carelessness and low notions of moral responsibility.

The beau-ideal of school discipline with regard to young boys would appear to be this—that whilst corporal punishment was retained on principle as fitly answering to, and marking the naturally inferior state of boyhood, morally and intellectually, and therefore as conveying no peculiar degradation to persons in such a state, we should cherish and encourage to the utmost all attempts made by the several boys as individuals to escape from the natural punishment of their age by rising above its naturally low tone of principle. While we told them, that, as being boys, they were not degraded by being punished as boys, we should tell them also, that in proportion as we saw them trying to anticipate their age morally, so we should delight to anticipate it also in our treatment of them personally—that every approach to the steadiness of principle shown in manhood should be considered as giving a claim to the respectability of manhood—that we should be delighted to forget the inferiority of their age, as they laboured to lessen their moral and intellectual inferiority. This would be a discipline truly generous and wise, in one word, truly Christian—making an increase of dignity the certain consequence of increased virtuous effort, but giving no countenance to that barbarian pride which claims the treatment of a freeman and an equal, while it cherishes all the carelessness, the folly, and the low and selfish principle of a slave.

With regard to older boys, indeed, who yet have not attained that rank in the school which exempts them from corporal punishment, the question is one of greater difficulty. In this case the obvious objections to such a punishment are serious; and the truth is, that if a boy above fifteen is of such a character as to require flogging, the essentially trifling nature of school correction is inadequate to the offence. But in fact boys, after a certain age, who cannot keep their proper rank in a school, ought not to be retained at it; and if they do stay, the question becomes only a choice of evils. For the standard of attainment at a large school being necessarily adapted for no more than the average rate of capacity, a boy who, after fifteen, continues to fall below it, is either intellectually incapable of deriving benefit from the system of the place, or morally indisposed to do so, and in either case he ought to be removed from it.

And as the growth of the body is often exceedingly vigorous where that of the mind is slow, such boys are at once apt for many kinds of evil, and hard to be governed by moral motives, while they have outgrown the fear of school correction. There are fit subjects for private tuition, where the moral and domestic influences may be exercised upon them more constantly and personally than is compatible with the numbers of a large school. Meanwhile such boys, in fact, often continue to be kept at school by their parents, who would regard it as an inconvenience to be required to withdraw them. Now it is superfluous to say, that in these cases corporal punishment should be avoided wherever it is possible; and perhaps it would be best, if for such grave offences as would fitly call for it in younger boys, older boys whose rank in the school renders them equally subject to it, were at once to be punished by expulsion. As it is, the long-continued use of personal correction as a proper school punishment renders it possible to offer the alternative of flogging to an older boy, without subjecting him to any excessive degradation, and his submission to it marks appropriately the greatness and disgraceful character of his offence, while it establishes, at the same time, the important principle, that as long as a boy remains at school, the respectability and immunities of manhood must be earned by manly conduct and a manly sense of duty.

It seems to me, then, that the complaints commonly brought against our system of school discipline are wrong either in their principle or as to the truth of the fact. The complaint against *all* corporal punishment, as degrading and improper, goes, I think, upon a false and mischievous principle: the complaint against governing boys by fear, and mere authority, without any appeal to their moral feelings, is perfectly just in the abstract, but perfectly inapplicable to the actual state of schools in England.

By 'the power of fagging', I understand a power given by the supreme authorities of a school to the boys of the highest class or classes in it, to be exercised by them over the lower boys for the sake of securing the advantages of regular government amongst the boys themselves, and avoiding the evils of anarchy,—in other words, of the lawless tyranny of physical strength. This is the simple statement of the nature and ends of public school fagging —an institution which, like all other government, has been often abused and requires to be carefully watched, but which is as indispensable to a multitude of boys living together, as government, in like circumstances, is indispensable to a multitude of men.

I have said that fagging is necessary for a multitude of boys when *living together*; for this will show how the system may be required in the public schools of England, and yet be wholly needless in those of Scotland. The great Scotch schools are day-schools—those of England are boarding-schools. Now the difference between these two systems is enormous. In the Scotch schools the boys live at their own homes, and are under the government of their own relations; they only meet at school for a certain definite object during a certain portion of the day. But in England the boys, for nearly nine months of the year, live with one another in a distinct society; their school life occupies the whole of their existence; at their studies and at their amusements, by day and by night, they are members of one and the same society, and in closer local neighbourhood with one another than is the case with the ordinary society of grown men. At all those times, then, when Scotch boys are living at home in their respective families, English boys are living together amongst themselves alone; and for this their habitual living they require a government. It is idle to say that the masters form, or can form, this government; it is impossible to have a sufficient number of masters for the purpose; for, in order to obtain the advantages of home government, the boys should be as much divided as they are at their respective homes. There should be no greater number of schoolfellows living under one master than of brothers commonly living under one parent; nay, the number should be less, inasmuch as there is wanting that bond of natural affection which so greatly facilitates domestic government, and gives it its peculiar virtue. Even a father with thirty sons all below the age of manhood, and above childhood, would find it no easy matter to govern them effectually—how much less can a master govern thirty boys, with no natural bond to attach them either to him or to one another? He may indeed superintend their government of one another; he may govern them through their own governors; but to govern them immediately and at the same time effectively, is, I believe, impossible. And hence, if you have a large *boarding*-school, you cannot have it adequately governed without a system of fagging.

Now, a government among the boys themselves being necessary, the actual constitution of public schools places it in the best possible hands. Those to whom the power is committed are not simply the strongest boys, nor the oldest, nor yet the cleverest; they are those who have risen to the highest form in the school—that is to say, they will be probably at once the oldest, and the strongest, and the cleverest; and further, if the school be well ordered, they will be the most respectable in application and general character—those who have made the best use of the opportunities which the school affords, and are most capable of entering into its objects. In short, they constitute a real aristocracy, a government of the most worthy, their rank itself being an argument of their deserving. And their business is to keep order amongst the boys; to put a stop to improprieties of conduct, especially to prevent that oppression and ill-usage of the weaker boys by the stronger which is so often ignorantly confounded with a system of fagging. For all these purposes a general authority over the rest of the school is given them; and in some schools they have the power, like the masters, of enforcing this authority by impositions, that is, by setting tasks to be written out or learnt by heart for any misbehaviour. And this authority is exercised over all those boys who are legally subject to it, that is, over all below a certain place in the school, whatever be their age or physical strength; so that many boys who, if there were no regular fagging, would by mere physical force be exercising power over their school-fellows, although from their idleness, ignorance, and low principle they might be most unfit to do so, are now not only hindered from tyrannizing over others, but are themselves subject to authority—a most wholesome example, and one particularly needed at school, that mere physical strength, even amongst boys, is not to enjoy an ascendancy. Meanwhile this governing part of the school, thus invested with great responsibility, treated by the masters with great confidence and consideration, and being constantly in direct communication with the head master, and receiving their instruction almost exclusively from him, learn to feel a corresponding self-respect in the best sense of the term; they look upon themselves as answerable for the character of the school, and by the natural effect of their position acquire a manliness of mind and habits of conduct infinitely superior, generally speaking, to those of young men of the same age who have not enjoyed the same advantages.

What becomes then of those terrible stories of cruelty which inspire so many parents with horror at the very name of fagging; or what shall we say of that very representation of the fagging at Winchester, which appeared in the last Number of your Journal? It is confessed, indeed, in a subsequent page of that Number, that your correspondent's representation is not applicable to the present state of Winchester. Would it not then have been fairer to have inserted in the running title of the article, 'Flogging and Fagging at Winchester', the words, 'as formerly practised'? But, indeed, even as describing a past state of things, there is surely some confusion in the statement. It is important to distinguish such acts of oppression as belong properly to the system of fagging, from such as arise merely from superior physical force, and consequently exist as much, I believe a thousand times more, in those schools where there is no legal fagging. For instance, your correspondent complains of the tyranny practised at Winchester at bed-time, 'tossing in the blanket, tying toes, bolstering, etc.' These, indeed, are most odious practices, but what have they to do with fagging? I have known them to exist at private schools, where there was no fagging, to a degree of intolerable cruelty. In college, at Winchester, where there were two or three prefects in every chamber, I scarcely remember them to have been practised at all during the period of which I can speak from my own experience. And this is natural; for the boys who delight in this petty tyranny are very rarely to be found amongst the oldest in a school, and still less amongst those who have raised themselves to the highest rank in it: they are either middle-aged boys, from fourteen to sixteen, or such older boys as never distinguish themselves for any good, and who, never rising high in the school, are by a system of fagging, and by that only, restrained from abusing their size and strength in tyranny. Other abuses which your correspondent mentions, such as toasting, lighting fires, etc., arise so far from a system of fagging, that this system, when ill-regulated, allows a certain well-defined class of boys to exact services which otherwise would be exacted merely by the strongest. But I said, what every one must be aware of, that the government of boys, like every other government, requires to be watched, or it will surely be guilty of abuses. Those menial offices which were exacted from the juniors at Winchester were only required of them because the attendance of servants was so exceedingly insufficient, and the accommodations of the boys in many particulars so greatly neglected. If you do not provide servants to clean the boys' shoes, to supply them with water of a morning, or to wait on them at their meals, undoubtedly the more powerful among them, whether the power be natural or artificial, will get these things done for them by the weaker; but supply the proper attendance, and all this ceases immediately. There will remain many miscellaneous services, such as watching for balls at cricket or fives, carrying messages, etc., which servants undoubtedly cannot be expected always to perform, and which yet belong to that general authority vested in the boys of the highest form. They belong to that general authority, and are therefore now claimed as rightfully due; but if there were no such authority, they would be claimed by the stronger from the weaker. For I assume it as a certain fact, that if you have two or three hundred boys living with one another as a distinct society, there will be some to command, as in all other societies, and others to obey: the only difference is, that the present system first of all puts the power into the best hands; and, secondly, by recognising it as legal, is far better able to limit its exercise and to prevent its abuses, than it could be if the whole were a mere irregular dominion of the stronger over the weaker.

There is another thing, which to those who are acquainted with schools, will seem of no small importance. Leave a number of boys together as legally equal, and the irregular tyranny exercised under these circumstances by every stronger boy over every weaker one, has so far the sanction of the public opinion of the school, that any individual sufferer would be utterly afraid to complain of his ill usage to the master. But give one class a legal superiority over the rest, and an abuse of power on their part is no longer received with sympathy; and the boy who were to complain of it to the master, instead of being hated as an informer, would rather be regarded by the mass of his companions as an asserter of their common liberties. Now to those who consider the difficulty of getting boys to complain of ill usage where public opinion condemns the complaining, it will appear an immense security against oppression, that it may be denounced without incurring general odium; and such I fear is the Jacobinical spirit of human nature, that this can never be the case unless the oppression proceed from one invested with *legal* authority.

For my own part, however, I am not one of those who think it an evil that younger or less manly boys should be subject legally to those more advanced in age and in character. Such subjection is not degrading, for it is rendered not to an arbitrary, but to a real superiority; it is shown to a power exercised in the main not for its own good, but for that of the society as a whole. Neither do I regard it as oppressive; for the degree and kind of obedience enforced under a well-regulated system of fagging is beneficial to those who pay it. A strict system is not therefore a cruel one; and the discipline to which boys are thus subjected, and the quickness, handiness, thoughtfulness, and punctuality, which they learn from some of the services required of them, are no despicable part of education. Many a man who went from Winchester to serve in the Peninsula in the course of the last war must have found his school experience and habits no bad preparation for the activity and hardships of a campaign; not only in the mere power of endurance, but in the helpfulness and independence which his training as a junior had given him. When your correspondent talks of the servility encouraged by the system of fagging, and gravely imputes to this cause what he calls the characteristic servility of English gentlemen, the cause appears to me as wrongly assigned as I think the supposed result imaginary.

The real servility which exists in England, whether amongst men or boys, is not an excessive deference for legal authority, but a surrender of individual judgement and conscience to the tyranny of public opinion. This tyranny exists in schools to a fatal degree; but it is not exercised chiefly by those who have the power of fagging, and far less in virtue of that power; on the contrary, the boys of the highest form are the only corrective of it, and so far as they contribute to it, it is not owing to the power which distinguishes them from the other boys, but to that imperfection of age and judgement which, to a certain degree, they share in common with them. Great, indeed, is this evil; but it is one arising almost inevitably from the circumstances of a *boarding*-school, namely, that it is a society wholly composed of persons whose state, morally and intellectually, is, by reason of their age, exceedingly imperfect.

It is this which renders it so difficult to make a large school a place of Christian education. For while, on the one hand, the boys stand to their masters in the relation of pupils to a teacher, they form, on the other hand, a complete society amongst themselves; and the individual boys, while influenced by him in the one relation, are unhappily in the other more influenced by that whole of which they are members, and which affects them in a much larger portion of their lives. And how can this influence be of a Christian character, when the perfect impression of Christianity cannot possibly be received by any society which is not in the highest state of advancement? by all others it is either taken incorrectly, or repelled altogether:

they can but exhibit that mixture of superstition and profaneness which characterized the semi-barbarous societies of the middle ages; a mixture as unfavourable to the development of a man's highest excellence, as Christianity purely imbibed is favourable to it, and indispensable.

The stress of this remark, however, applies to a *society* in a low moral state, and not to an individual. Boys in their own families, as members of the natural and wholesome society of their father's household, may receive its lessons, and catch its spirit, and learn at a very early age to estimate right and wrong truly. But a society formed exclusively of boys, that is, of elements each separately weak and imperfect, becomes more than an aggregate of their several defects: the amount of evil in the mass is more than the sum of the evil in the individuals; it is aggravated in its character, while the amount of good, on the contrary, is less in the mass than in the individuals, and its effect greatly weakened.

Now this being the case, and the very fact of a *boarding-*school involving the existence of such an unfavourable state of society, he who wishes really to improve public education would do well to direct his attention to this point; and to consider how there can be infused into a society of boys such elements as, without being too dissimilar to coalesce thoroughly with the rest, shall yet be so superior as to raise the character of the whole. It would be absurd to say that any school has as yet fully solved this problem. I am convinced, however, that in the peculiar relation of the highest form to the rest of the boys, such as it exists in our great public schools, there is to be found the best means of answering it. This relation requires in many respects to be improved in its character; some of its features should be softened, others elevated: but here and here only is the engine which can effect the end desired; and if *boarding-*schools are to be cleared of their most besetting faults and raised in all that is excellent, it must be done by a judicious improvement; but most assuredly not by the abolition of the system of authorized fagging. [*QJEd*, vol. IX, No. XVIII, 1835, pp. 281–92. Also reproduced in *MW*.]

Idleness, extravagance and other temptations of public schools

We all know the terms of reproach and ridicule which are thrown out against a boy who works in earnest and upon principle. He is laughed at for taking unnecessary trouble, for being afraid of punishment, or for wishing to gain favour with his masters, and be thought by them to be better than other boys. Either of these reproaches is one which a boy finds it very hard to bear—he does not like to be thought afraid, or plodding, or as wishing to court favour. He has not age or sense, or firmness enough to know and to answer, that the only fear of which he need be ashamed is the fear of his equals, the fear of those who are in no respect better than himself, and have therefore no sort of right to direct him. To be afraid then of other boys is, in a boy, the same sort of weakness as it is in a man to be afraid of other men: and as a man ought to be equally ashamed of fearing men and of not fearing God, so a boy ought to be ashamed of fearing boys, and also to be ashamed of not fearing his parents and instructors. Amongst boys the fear of their parents and teachers will only make them manly, and noble, and high spirited, but the fear of their companions leads them to everything low, and childish, and contemptible. Those boys, then, who try to make others idle, and laugh at them for trying to please their masters, are exactly like the men who laugh at their neighbours for being religious, and for living in the fear of God: and both are like the more hardened ruffians in a gang of thieves or other criminals, whose amusement it is to laugh at the fear of justice, which beginners in crime have not yet quite got over. In all these instances there is not only the guilt of our own sin, but the far worse guilt of encouraging sin in others; and, as I showed you last Sunday how your school faults, although very trifling in their worldly consequences, were yet as serious in the sight of God as the faults of grown men.

Again, with regard to Extravagance, and the breach of school regulations. There are some boys who, remembering the wishes of their parents, are extremely unwilling to incur debts, and to spend a great deal of money upon their own eating, and drinking, and amusements. There are some too, who, knowing that the use of wine or any liquor of that sort is forbidden, because the use of it among boys is sure to be the abuse of it, would not wish to indulge in anything of the kind themselves. But they are assailed by the example, and the reproaches, and the laughter of others. It is mean, and poor spirited, and ungenerous, not to contribute to the pleasures and social enjoyments of their companions; in short, not to do as others do. The charge of stinginess, of not spending his money liberally, is one which a boy is particularly sore at hearing. He forgets that in his case such a charge is the greatest possible folly. Where is the generosity of spending money which is not your own, and which as soon as it is spent, is to be supplied again with no sacrifice on your part? Where is the stinginess of not choosing to beg money of your dearest friends, in order to employ it in a manner which those friends would disapprove of?—for, after all, the money must come from them, as you have it not, nor can you earn it for yourselves. But there is another laugh behind: a boy is laughed at for being kept so strictly at home that he cannot get money as he likes, and he is taught to feel ashamed and angry at the hard restraint which is laid upon him. Truly that boy has gone a good way in the devil's service,

who will dare to set another against his father and his
mother, who will teach him that their care and authority
are things which he should be ashamed of. Of those who
can do this, well may Christ say, that 'it were better for
them that a millstone were tied about their neck and that
they were drowned in the depth of the sea'. You who are
laughed at because you will not be idle, or drunken, or
extravagant, or undutiful, or in some way or other base
and low principled—beware lest you are laughed and
frightened out of your eternal salvation. [*Sermons*, vol. 2,
pp. 51–3.]

*The relative values in school of idleness, industry and
perseverance*

In the true scale of excellence, moral perfection is most
highly valued, then comes excellence of understanding,
and, last of all, strength and activity of body. But at school
this is just reversed. A strong and active boy is very much
respected; a clever boy is also admired;—but a good and
well-principled boy meets with very little encouragement.
Again, natural abilities are admired and valued; but it is
the tendency of many persons to admire them much less
when united with sound sense and industry than when they
are to be found in one who does not cultivate them, but
abuses them by his indolence, or by converting them to
some purpose of wickedness or folly. It is indeed remarkable, that nowhere else is the habitual breach of our duty
so countenanced as it is here. A soldier who was notoriously
idle and cowardly would not only be punished by his
superiors, but would be an object of dislike and contempt
to his comrades themselves. But here, on the contrary,
idleness is with many rather a glory, and industry is
considered as a reproach. When a boy first comes from
home, full of the natural desire of doing his duty, of
improving himself, and getting on well, he is presently

beset by the ridicule of all the worthless and foolish boys around him, who want to sink him to their own level. How completely true is it, that his foes are they of his own household;—that is, they who are most immediately about him, those of his own age, and his own place in the school. They become his idol: before their most foolish, most low, and most wicked voices, he gives up his affections, his understanding, and his conscience: from this mass of ignorance, and falsehood, and selfishness, he looks for the guide of his opinions and his conduct.

There are some dispositions which, from absolute indolence, seem to be zealous about nothing whatever;—persons who appear neither to care about business or pleasure, who cannot be roused to take an active interest in anything. These are characters which exist, and which we must all have sometimes met with: but they are not common, neither are they very dangerous, because the general feeling of men is apt to despise them as stupid and insensible. A much more common case is that of persons who like some things exceedingly, and are all alive whenever they happen to be engaged in them; but who do not like their common employment, and display about that no interest at all. This is a very common case, for it rarely happens that our employment is the very one which we should most choose, or the one which we most choose at this particular time, or under these particular circumstances. We all know that the expectation of any great pleasure is apt to unsettle our minds: although our work may commonly interest us tolerably, yet now, with this prospect before us, it seems dull and tiresome; we regard it merely as a burden, and grudge every hour that we give to it. So then, it seems that we must all expect to have our work often disagreeable to us, and that in many cases it is always disagreeable; disagreeable I mean by nature, and speaking according to common notions. But to say that a man can do heartily what is disagreeable to him, is to talk of impossibilities; he can no more do it than he can have an appetite for nauseous food: he will attend to what he dislikes no more than he can help; and, so far from following it up so earnestly as to allow himself no leisure so much as to eat, he will be glad of every excuse, and enlarge as much as possible upon the claims of his health, his strength, and his reasonable liberty, in order to abridge to the utmost the time, which he cannot altogether refuse, to what he knows to be the call of duty.

It may be said, then, that I have given the idle all the excuse they can desire; for I say that no one *can* do heartily what is disagreeable to him, and they will maintain very truly that their daily employment *is* disagreeable to them. I know that it is so; but it does not follow that it must always *remain so*. True it is, that we cannot do heartily what we dislike; but it is no less true that we may learn if we will to like many things which we at present dislike: and the real guilt of idleness consists in its refusal to go through this discipline. I might speak of the well-known force of habit, in reconciling us to what is most unwelcome to us; that by mere perseverance what was at first very hard, becomes first a little less so, then much less so, and at last so easy that, according to a well-known law of our faculties, it becomes a pleasure to them to do it. But although perseverance will certainly do this, yet what is to make us so persevering?—if we go through this discipline it will cure us, but what can engage us to give it a fair trial? [*Sermons*, vol. 2, pp. 104–5; 160–1.]

Idleness and the English gentleman

I often think that nothing could so rouse a boy's energies as sending him out to you [i.e. to Van Dieman's Land, the present Tasmania] where he must work or starve. There is no earthly thing more mean and despicable in my mind than an English gentleman destitute of all sense of his responsibilities and opportunities, and only revelling in the luxuries of our high civilisation, and thinking himself a great person. [*SL*, ccxxxv, 12 April 1840, p. 554.]

The distracting nature of the new popular books and serialised literature

Childishness in boys, even of good abilities, seems to me to be a growing fault, and I do not know to what to ascribe it, except to the great number of exciting books of amusement, like Pickwick and Nickleby, Bentley's Magazine, etc. etc. These completely satisfy all the intellectual appetite of a boy, which is rarely very voracious, and leave him totally palled, not only for his regular work, which I could well excuse in comparison, but for good literature of all sorts, even for History and for Poetry. [*SL*, ccii, 6 July 1839, p. 511.]

The works of amusement published only a very few years since were comparatively few in number;[11] they were less exciting, and therefore less attractive; they were dearer, and therefore less accessible; and, not being published periodically, they did not occupy the mind for so long a time, nor keep alive so constant an expectation; nor, by thus dwelling upon the mind, and distilling themselves into it as it were drop by drop, did they possess it so largely, colouring even, in many instances, its very language, and affording frequent matter for conversation.

The evil of all these circumstances is actually enormous. The mass of human minds, and much more of the minds of young persons, have no great appetite for intellectual exercise; but they have some, which by careful treatment may be strengthened and increased. But here to this weak and delicate appetite is presented an abundance of the most stimulating and least nourishing food possible. It snatches it greedily, and is not only satisfied, but actually conceives a distaste for anything simpler and more whole-some. That curiosity which is wisely given us to lead us on to knowledge, finds its full gratification in the details of an exciting and protracted story, and then lies down as it were gorged, and goes to sleep. Other faculties claim their turn, and have it. We know that in youth the healthy body and lively spirits require exercise, and in this they may and ought to be indulged; but the time and interest which remain over when the body has had its enjoyment, and the mind desires its share, this has been already wasted and exhausted upon things utterly unprofitable: so that the mind goes to its work hurriedly and languidly, and feels it to be no more than a burden. The mere lessons may be learnt from a sense of duty; but that freshness of power, which in young persons of ability would fasten eagerly upon some one portion or other of the wide field of know-ledge, and there expatiate, drinking in health and strength to the mind, as surely as the natural exercise of the body gives to it bodily vigour,—that is tired prematurely, per-verted, and corrupted; and all the knowledge which else it might so covet, it now seems a wearying effort to attain.

Great and grievous as is the evil, it is peculiarly hard to find the remedy for it. If the books to which I have been alluding were books of downright wickedness, we might destroy them wherever we found them; we might forbid their open circulation; we might conjure you to shun them as you would any other clear sin, whether of word or deed. But they are not wicked books for the most part; they are of that class which cannot be actually prohibited; nor can it be pretended that there is a sin in reading them. They are not the more wicked for being published so cheap, and at regular intervals; but yet these two circumstances make them so peculiarly injurious. All that can be done is to point out the evil; that it is real and serious I am very sure, and its effects are most deplorable on the minds of the fairest promise; but the remedy for it rests with yourselves, or rather with each of you individually, so far as he is himself concerned. That an unnatural and constant excitement of the mind is most injurious, there is no doubt; that excitement involves a consequent weakness, is a law of our nature than which none is surer; that the weakness of mind thus produced is and must be adverse to quiet study and thought, to that reflection which alone is wisdom, is also clear in itself, and proved too largely by experience. [*Sermons*, vol. 4, pp. 39–42.]

The constant threat of ill health to a school's prosperity

The amount of fever in Rugby is but trifling; but if a single boy were to catch it, after the two fatal cases of last half-year, the panic would be so great that we should not be able to keep the school together, or to reassemble it till after Christmas. [*SL*, CCLXXIX, 1 September 1841, p. 610.]

THE FUTURE OCCUPATIONS OF BOYS

The dangers of a career in the Army and Navy; the need for the good opinion of the world often swamps the greater moral issues involved

Officers of the Army and Navy have, I fear, often fatally deceived themselves: they think sometimes, that in their profession, if they are regular in attending and enforcing the attendance of their men at divine service on a Sunday, —if they avoid swearing and profane language, and try to keep up respect to religion and its ministers amongst those under their command or influence,—they may safely consider themselves as true Christians. But he is a Christian, who, for the love of Christ, and with prayer for the help of Christ's Spirit, struggles against the besetting temptations of his particular calling. And in the world in general, but most especially in the Army and Navy, the great and besetting temptation is to prefer the praise of men to the praise of God, and to dread the reproach of men more than the reproach of God. Where this feeling is not earnestly struggled with, it obtains in a short time such a dominion, that we shall certainly act in every point as it leads us. The most degrading personal cowardice is not so complete a bondage as the cowardice which fears to be called coward. The most timid man alive would be ashamed to say, and to accustom himself to think, that if he were placed in a situation of danger, he must fly from it. However fearful his nature, he would struggle against his weakness, and pray earnestly, and earnestly labour, that if he were to be tried with severe pain and danger, they might not overpower his firmness; and there are many instances of persons, constitutionally timid, thus bracing themselves, and being supported by God; so that their resolution has endured amidst the most appalling dangers and the most fearful torments. But moral cowardice,—or the fear of what man can do, not to kill the body, but to inflict shame and insult on the mind,—men do not scruple to confess that they would yield to. They will expose their own lives, and risk taking away the lives of others, in personal quarrels, because they have been accustomed to set such a value on the good opinion of the world, that the temptation of dishonour is one which they are not strong enough to resist.

For those, then, who are soon going to enter upon active life, the most earnest prayer that I would urge them to make to God on this solemn occasion, is, that He would enable them to overcome this most fearful temptation, the dread of the censure or dishonour of the world. [Sermons, vol. 2, pp. 215–16.]

If then there be any here who are thinking of becoming soldiers or sailors, let me conjure them to examine well their own hearts, and to remember whose pledged soldiers they are already. If true to that service, and judging soberly of their own particular faculties, they think that Christ's call, as signified by the nature of His gifts to them, invites them to serve Him in an active life, where the bolder and harder virtues will be most exercised, let them not fear to obey the call: but rather let them bear earnestly in mind that He is calling them, and let them never cease to follow Him. But if it be idleness, impatience of restraint or work here, a foolish vanity, or a sinful carelessness that prompts them; and if they dread the yoke of Christ, and think that as soldiers or sailors they will be less required to take it upon them,—then let them be assured that God's curse is on their heart's desire so cherished; that their thought is not of faith, but of unbelief and wickedness; that they are devoting themselves without a struggle to the service of sin and of death. It is vain for them, and is no more than self-deceit; to ask advice of their friends in such a matter: their friends cannot see into their hearts, nor judge from what motives their desire of any particular profession may arise. But you can judge of yourselves; and you are to judge at your own peril. [*Sermons*, vol. 3, p. 146.]

The scattering of boys to the distant parts of the empire and their duty

But our congregation will of necessity within a few years be all scattered to the four winds of heaven; we should look for its several members anywhere rather than here. Again, take even a congregation such as ours in any other country, and although we know that in a short time it will be dispersed from the place where we actually behold it, yet still it will be dispersed only within narrow limits, the limits of the country to which it belongs. But our country spreads forth her arms so widely that the scattering of the members of an English school, by the various circumstances of life, is literally a scattering over the whole habitable world; there is no distance so great to which it is not within probability that some of our congregation may betake themselves. And yet once again; those very distant countries, those ends of the earth to which some of us may in the course of things be led, are new settlements, with a small population, with institutions, habits and national character unformed as yet, and to be formed; unformed, and capable therefore in their unsettled state of being influenced greatly by the conduct and character even of a single individual, so that, putting all these things together, a stranger does well to feel something more than a common interest in the sight of the congregation assembled within this chapel, as it is this day. Now whatever occurs of unusual interest in the world strikes in this way upon an answering key within our breasts here. Whatever of striking good or of evil happens in any part of the wide range of English dominion, declares upon what important scenes some of you may be called upon to enter. And seeing and hearing the distant battle, is it not very natural to wish that those who may be called to take part in it should be well armed and well trained for the contest; that however trying may be the outward circumstances in which you will have to act, you may not be false to yourselves and to your duty; that you may be so armed with all a Christian's armour, as in all places and circumstances to do a Christian's part, worthily, wisely, and zealously, in doing and in bearing?

But one thing is clear; three parties there are concerned, of whose existence it behoves us to be equally and intensely conscious; three, and these three are God, on the one hand, and your own individual souls on the other, and the one Mediator Jesus Christ, who alone can join the two into one.[12] [*Sermons*, vol. 5, pp. 402–6.]

With regard to my children's worldly prospects I have no dread or dislike of colonisation, if they are strong enough in principle to bear the influence of so much lower a tone of morals.[13]

Richer classes of society are very content to send their sons to India in contrast to the alleged injustice of assisted emigration for the lower classes

I am at a loss to understand how it can be unjust or inhuman to say to a man who is here barely able to keep himself from starving, that we will assist him to go to another country, where he may live in comfort, and provide sufficiently for himself and his family. I know that such a proposal made to persons in the richer classes is not thought a hardship or an insult, but a great favour; that fathers are glad to get situations for their sons in

India, even though they part with them for such a number of years, that they cannot expect to live till they return. No doubt a parent would rather be able to provide for his son comfortably at home than send him to India; but he would much rather send him to India than see him live in beggary at home; and it does not occur to him to ask his neighbour to give him a piece of his estate, rather than that he should have to bear the pain of parting. Or if any particular trade be overstocked in any town, the man who finds himself best able to support himself by capital previously acquired, does not think himself injured if he be advised to go and look for an opening in his trade elsewhere. It is, indeed, a shocking thing that poor men should be persuaded to emigrate without knowing anything of the country to which they are going, and without having any one to advise them when they get there. And this ignorance, I am inclined to think, is one of the greatest obstacles to emigration. No man likes to take a leap in the dark; and emigration is nothing better than a leap in the dark, when a man has never before been ten miles from his own village, when he has no notion of distances, and knows not a single particular about the climate, productions, customs, and manner of living in foreign countries. A mere elementary knowledge of geography would instantly dispel the vague fears which many of the poor now feel unreasonably: emigration would thus lose its terrors, and their knowledge would not only make them cease to fear it, but would teach them how to derive the full benefit of it.

This is a subject which the Government have taken up, and on which I hope they will proceed to act on a large scale, as soon as the Reform question is once settled. Here, as everywhere else, the importance of increasing the knowledge of the poor forces itself upon us most strongly. Ignorance, indeed, meets us at every turn, as one of the greatest difficulties which we have to encounter. [*MW*, pp. 199–200.]

The professional way of life the only honest way of living

It is a real pleasure to me to find that you are taking steadily to a profession, without which I scarcely see how a man can live honestly. That is, I use the term 'profession' in rather a large sense, not as simply denoting certain callings which a man follows for his maintenance, but rather a definite field of duty, which the nobleman has as much as the tailor, but which he has not who, having an income large enough to keep him from starving, hangs about upon life, merely following his own caprices and fancies. [*SL*, CXLI, 31 October 1836, p. 422.]

Medicine and the law: their relative moral worth

Medicine, like Law, always attracted me as much in its study as it has repelled me in practice; not that I feel alike towards the practice of both; on the contrary I honour the one as much as I abhor [the other]:—moral nastiness, in which a lawyer lives and breathes, is far worse than objects physically repulsive: and then the physician meddles with physical evil in order to relieve and abate it; the lawyer meddles with moral evil rather to aggravate it than to mend. Yet the study of Law is, I think, glorious, transcending that of any earthly thing. [*SL*, CLXII, 18 September 1837, p. 455.][14]

The philosophy of medicine, I imagine, is almost at zero: our practice is empirical, and seems hardly more than a course of guessing, more or less happy. The theory of life itself lies probably beyond our knowledge. How ignorant are we of the causes of disorder, of the real influence of air, of infection, and of that strange phenomenon of diseases incident generally to the human frame,

such as measles, small-pox, and the old Athenian plague?
Here, and in a thousand other points, there is room for
infinite discoveries. [*SL*, cxxviii, 9 May 1836, pp. 405–6.]

*Although the clergy must come from the richer classes, they
are often not welcome and the situation is not healthy*

The established clergy must belong generally to the
richer classes, because so long as a residence at the university is a necessary passport to ordination, none but the
rich can afford to enter the Church. But separated as the
richer and poorer classes are from one another in England,
separated not only in manners, habits, and feelings, but
actually in language also, who can wonder if the poor
desire a religious instructor with whom they can more
nearly sympathize than with their regular clergyman,—
an instructor who by birth, station, language, and manners,
is more nearly one of themselves. True it is that when the
regular clergyman is at once a good man and a sensible
man, his being a gentleman is all so much in his favour; for
though a gentleman parson be a very bad thing if the
gentleman be the predominant element in the compound,
yet a good parson who in education and feeling is a
thorough gentleman beside, in the best sense of the word,
inspires justly a degree of respect and confidence as well
as of affection which the poor never can feel towards a
man of coarser manners and less education. But in the
nature of things there will be always a great many of the
clergy in whom the gentleman, *not in the best sense of the
word*, is predominant over the parson; and then as far as
the poor are concerned, the salt that had lost its savour was
not more worthless than they find such a minister. [*MW*,
pp. 224–5.]

THE UNIVERSITIES
[For a reference to the need for local universities see p. 96.]

OXFORD UNIVERSITY

The importance of being educated at Oxford

If you have got your views for your course of life into a definite shape, so as to see your way clear before you, and this course is wholly at variance with the studies of a University, then there is nothing to be said, except that I am sorry and surprised, and should be very anxious to learn what your views are. But if you look forward to any of what are called the learned professions, and wish still to carry on the studies of a well educated man, depend upon it that you are in the right place where you are [Oxford], and have greater means within your reach there, than you can readily obtain elsewhere. University distinctions are a great starting point in life; they introduce a man well, nay, they even add to his influence afterwards.

Consider that a young man has no means of becoming independent of the society about him. If you wish to exercise influence hereafter, begin by distinguishing yourself in the regular way, not by seeming to prefer a separate way of your own. [*SL*, LXXXV, 29 October 1834, pp. 339–40].

The desire for reform at Oxford is a measure of Arnold's love for it

It does not follow because one admires and loves the surpassing beauty of the place and its association, or because one forms in it the most valuable and most delightful friendships, that therefore one is to uphold its foolishnesses, and try to perpetuate its faults. My love for any place or person, or institution, is exactly the measure of my desire to reform them; a doctrine which seems to me as natural now, as it seemed strange when I was a child. [*SL*, xcv, 4 March 1835, p. 353.][15]

College standards are too low

And until the Universities have an examination upon admission, as a University, not a college regulation, the standard of the college lecture rooms will be so low, that a young man going from the top of a public school will be nearly losing his time, and tempted to go back in his scholarship by attending them. This is an old grievance at Oxford, as I can bear witness, when I myself was an undergraduate just come from Winchester. [*SL*, xci, 25 January 1835, p. 347.]

Dissenters should be admitted to the University

The undersigned members of the Universities of Oxford and Cambridge, many of them being engaged in education, entertaining a strong sense of the peculiar benefits to be derived from studying at the Universities, cannot but consider it as a national evil, that these benefits should be inaccessible to a large proportion of their countrymen.

While they feel most strongly that the foundation of all education must be laid in the great truths of Christianity, and would on no account consent to omit these, or to teach them imperfectly, yet they cannot but acknowledge, that these truths are believed and valued by the great majority of Dissenters, no less than by the Church of England; and that every essential point of Christian instruction may be communicated without touching on those particular questions on which the Church and the mass of Dissenters are at issue.

And, while they are not prepared to admit such Dissenters as differ from the Church of England on the most essential points of Christian truth, such as the modern Unitarians of Great Britain, they are of opinion, that all other Dissenters may be admitted into the Universities, and allowed to take degrees there with great benefit to the country, and to the probable advancement of Christian truth and Christian charity amongst members of all persuasions.[16]

A solution to the Unitarian problem at the University

My feeling about Unitarians is this, that they could not be included *at present* in the religious instruction of the colleges, without such omissions in that instruction as no good Church of England man would think it right to make:—on the other hand, if you allow them not to attend your religious instruction or religious worship, you seem to me to countenance what I certainly shrink from,—the separation of education from Christianity:— you stand to a person in loco parentis, and yet waive a parent's highest duty and privilege,—the instructing his child for eternity. This I think affects all such places of education as colleges and schools, where the tutors and masters have not only the charge of their pupils intellectually but morally.

But I should agree with you in admitting Unitarians to the university,—if the true university system were restored,—and it was not necessary in order to belong to the university, to belong to some now existing college or hall. I would then allow Unitarians to be at a hall or halls of their own, under their own instructors,—or of course allow them to enter at our colleges if they liked to attend our religious service and instructions;—and I would so far alter the examination statute, as to make the Divinity examination refer only to the evidences of Christianity generally, and the substance of the Old and New Testaments;—dismissing all examination in the 39 Articles.

I have long thought, on wholly independent grounds, that the restoration of the university, by allowing every Master of Arts to open a hall with the Chancellor's licence, and to receive students amenable to all the public discipline of the university besides his own domestic discipline within doors;—and by restoring the government to the proper university officers, i.e. the professors, or the doctors in the three faculties,—or a body chosen by them, without any reference whatever to the colleges, would be a most important improvement;—and nothing I think would so readily obviate the difficulties of the Dissenters' question. [Letter dated 7 May 1834. British Museum. Additional 34,589.64.][17]

Other reforms should involve the system of fines, the oaths, and the ability to open new halls of residence

There are three points at Oxford, which, though of very different importance, might all, I think, be noticed with advantage.

1st. The system of fines[18]—I do not mean as regards the tenant, but as regards those members of the College Foundations who do not belong to the governing body. It is the practice, I believe, to divide the Corn Rents either equally or in certain fixed proportions, fixed by the Founder, among all the members of the Foundation;— but the fines, which form always a large proportion of the gross income of the College, are divided exclusively by the governing body amongst themselves; where this governing body includes all the Fellows, as at Oriel, Corpus, and New College, then those who do not share the fines are only the Scholars and Probationer Fellows; but where it consists of what is called a seniority seven, or whatever number it be, of the senior Fellows, then all the Fellows not on the seniority are excluded; and this is the case at Brasenose. Now the question is, whether this is according to the Founder's intentions, or whether it has been legalised by any subsequent statute—of the realm, I mean, not of the University. The fines originally were a direct bribe paid by the tenant to the Bursar or Treasurer of the college, for letting him renew on favourable terms; subsequently the bursars were not allowed to keep it all to themselves, but it was shared by all those with whom lay the power of either granting or refusing the renewal. But still, if the college property be notoriously underlet, because a great part of the rent is paid in the shape of fines, those who are entitled to a certain share in the proceeds, are manifestly defrauded if they are not allowed their proportion of the fines also. This question only affects the members of the several foundations as individuals;—still it has always struck me as a great unfitness, that a system should go on with such a primâ facie look of direct fraud about it.

2nd. All members of foundations are required to take an oath to maintain the rights of the college, etc., and amongst other things they swear that if expelled by the college, they will not appeal to any court of law. This oath is imposed at Winchester College, or was in my time, on every boy as soon as he was fifteen. I object utterly, on principle, to any private society administering an oath to its members at all—still more so to boys. But even if it were a promise or engagement, the promise of not appealing to the King's Courts is monstrous, and savours completely of the spirit of secret societies, who regard the law as their worst enemy. The University has lately repealed some of its oaths—but still retains far too many.

3rd. The University should be restored—that is, the monopoly of the colleges should be taken away—by allowing any Master of Arts, according to the old practice of Oxford, to open a hall for the reception of students. The present practice dates, I think, from the age of Elizabeth— when the old halls had fallen into decay; and then the gift of the headship of the existing halls was placed in the Chancellor's hands, and every member of the University

was required to be a member of some college, or of one of
these recognised halls. The evils of the present system,
combined with a statute passed, I believe, within the
present century, obliging every undergraduate under three
years' standing to sleep in college, are very great. The
number of members at a college is regulated, therefore,
by the size of its building, and thus some of the very worst
colleges have the greatest number of votes in Convoca-
tion, and consequently the greatest influence in the
decisions of the University. [*SL*, CLIV, 8 March 1837,
pp. 441–3.][19]

If Roman Catholics, as such, had a college of their own at
Oxford, I do not believe that there would be half the dis-
puting or proselytising which exists now, where Roman
Catholic opinions are held by men calling themselves
members of our Church. [*SL*, CCLXVIII, 4 April 1842,
p. 594, from a letter about the college in Van Diemen's
Land; see p. 166.]

LONDON UNIVERSITY

*Arnold's dilemma in his London University appointment—
the necessity for fusing national and christian education and
the prevention of the establishment of more sectarian places
of education*

The '*Idea*' of my life, to which I think every thought of
my mind more or less tends, is the perfecting the 'idea'
of the Edward the Sixth Reformers,—the constructing a
truly national and Christian Church, and a truly national
and Christian system of education. The more immediate
question now is, with regard to the latter. The Address
of the House of Commons about the London University,
is to be answered by appointing a body of Examiners by
Royal Charter, with power to confer Degrees in Arts,

Law, and Medicine, on students of the London University and of King's College, and of such other places of education as the Crown from time to time may name. I have accepted the office of one of the Examiners in Arts,—not without much hesitation, and many doubts of the success of the plan, but desirous, if possible, to exercise some influence on a measure which seems to me full of very important consequences for good or for evil. Before I knew any thing about this, I had written a pamphlet on the Admission of Dissenters into the Universities; not meaning to publish it directly, if at all; but wishing to embody my view of the whole question, in which, of course, I take the deepest interest. Now, if I act with this new Board, I am more disposed to publish my own views for my own justification, lest any man should think me an advocate for the plan of National Education without Christianity; which I utterly abhor. But I am well nigh driven beside myself, when I think that to this monstrosity we are likely to come; because the zealots of different sects, (including in this term the Establishment, pace Archiepiscopi Cantuarensis,) will have no Christianity without Sectarianism. [*SL*, CXII, 18 November 1835, pp. 386–7.]

I hold myself bound to prevent, so far as in me lies, the establishment of more sectarian places of education, which will be the case if you have regular colleges for Dissenters; and yet Dissenters must and ought to have Degrees; and you shut them out from Oxford and Cambridge. No man can feel more strongly than I do the necessary imperfection of the proposed system, and its certain inferiority to what the old Universities might be made, or even to what they are, I suppose, actually. No man can more dread the cooperators with whom I may possibly have to work, or the principle which an active party are endeavouring to

carry into education, that it shall or can exist independent
of Christianity. But the excuse of these men, and their
probable success, arises out of the Oxford sectarianism.
You have identified Christianity with the Church of
England, and—as there are many who will not bear the
latter,—indifferent men, or unbelievers, believe that it
must follow that they cannot be taught the former. The
question goes through the whole frame of our society.
Nothing more reasonable than that national education
should be in accordance with the national religion;
nothing more noble or more wise in my judgement than
the whole theory of the Reformers on this point. But the
Established Church is only the religion of a part of the
nation, and there is the whole difficulty. The Reformers,
or rather their successors in Elizabeth's time, wished to
root out Dissent by the strong hand. This was wicked, as
I think, as well as foolish: but then, if we do not root out
Dissent, and so keep the Establishment co-extensive with
the nation, we must extend the Establishment, or else in
the end there will and ought to be no Establishment at all,
which I consider as one of the greatest of all evils. [*SL*,
cxiii, 4 November 1835, pp. 388–9.]

*London University's charter expressly infers christian and
moral education*

I need not say that I cordially agree with the principle of
the University that it recognises no sectarian distinctions.
But while I fully allow this, I also find it expressly de-
clared in our charter, that we are founded for the advancement of 'Religion and Morality'. And this seems to lead
to the exact conclusion which I most earnestly approve
of, that we are to be a Christian University, but not a
Romanist one, nor a Protestant, neither exclusively Church
of England, nor exclusively Dissenting. 'Religion', in
the king's mouth, can mean only Christianity; in fact, no

Christian can use it in any other sense without manifest inconsistency. Again, must it not follow that if we enter at all upon moral science, whether it be Moral Philosophy or History, we must be supposed to have some definite notions of moral truth? [*SL*, CLVIII, 30 April 1837, p. 449.]

Degrees in those Arts dealing with humanity involve christianity: a practical way of examining students with differing views of christianity

I have no wish to have Degrees in Divinity conferred by the London University, or to have a Theological Faculty; I am quite content with Degrees in Art. But then, let us understand what Arts are.

If *Arts* mean merely logic, or grammar, or arithmetic, or natural science, then, of course, a degree in Arts implies nothing whatever as to a man's moral judgement or principles. But open the definition a little farther—include poetry, or history, or moral philosophy—and you encroach unavoidably on the domain of moral education; and moral education cannot be separated from religious education, unless people have the old superstitious notion of religion, either that it relates to rites and ceremonies, or to certain abstract and unpractical truths. But, meaning by Religion what the Gospel teaches one to mean by it, it is nothing more nor less than a system directing and influencing our conduct, principles and feelings, and professing to do this with sovereign authority and most efficacious influence. If, then, I enter on the domain of moral knowledge, I am thereby on the domain of religious knowledge; and the only question is, what religion am I to follow? If I take no notice of the authority and influences of Christianity, I unavoidably take a view of man's life and principles from which they are excluded, that is, a view which acknowledges some other authority and influence—it may be of some other religion, or of some philosophy, or of mere

common opinion or instinct—but, in any case, I have one
of the many views of life and conduct which it was the very
purpose of Christ's coming into the world to exclude. And
how can any Christian man lend himself to the propagat-
ing or sanctioning a system of moral knowledge which
assumes that Christ's law is not our rule, nor His promises
our motive of action? This, then, is my principle, that
moral studies not based on Christianity must be un-
christian, and therefore are such as I can take no part
in.

On the other hand, I allow, as fully as you can do, that
the University should include Christians of every denomination without the slightest distinction. The differences
between Christian and Christian are not moral differences,
except accidentally. An Unitarian, as such, is a Christian—
that is, if a man follows Christ's law, and believes His
words according to his conscientious sense of their meaning, he is a Christian. But I believe—if I err as to the
matter of fact I shall greatly rejoice—that Unitarianism
happens to contain many persons who are only Unitarians
negatively, as not being Trinitarians; and I question
whether these follow Christ with enough of sincerity and
obedience to entitle them to be called Christians.

But it is an experiment undoubtedly worth trying,
whether, for the sake of upholding the Christian character
of our University, we ought not to venture on ground, new
indeed in England just at present, but which is of the very
essence of true Christianity. With all Christians except
Roman Catholics the course is plain, namely, to examine
every candidate for a degree in one of the Gospels and one
of the Epistles out of the Greek Testament. I would ask
of every man the previous question, 'To what denomination of Christians do you belong?' and according to his
answer I would specially avoid touching on those points
on which I, as a Churchman, differed from him. I should

probably say to him aloud, if the examination were public, 'Now I know that you and I differ on such and such points, and therefore I shall not touch on them; but we have a great deal more on which we agree, and therefore I may ask you so and so.' With the Roman Catholics there might be a difficulty, because they might possibly object to being examined by heretics, or in the Scriptures; but if so, where would be the difficulty of adding a Catholic to the number of Fellows on purpose for this object? or where would be the difficulty of requiring from the candidate, being a Catholic, a certificate of proficiency in religious knowledge from his own priest or bishop? [SL, CLV, 15 March 1837, pp. 443–5.][20]

Which comes first—national education or pandering to Jews and others?

Now, are we really for the sake of a few Jews, who may like to have a Degree in Arts—for the sake of one or two Mahommedans, who may possibly have the same wish, or for the sake of English unbelievers, who dare not openly avow themselves—are we to destroy our only chance of our being even either useful or respected as an institution of national education? There is no difficulty with Dissenters of any denomination; what we have proposed has been so carefully considered, that it is impossible to pretend that it bears a sectarian character; it is objected to merely as being Christian, as excluding Jews, Turks, and misbelievers. [SL, CLXIII, 18 November 1837, p. 456.]

The christian problems of London University and the position and standing of the college in Gower Street

The whole question turns upon this—whether the University of London was to be open to all Christians without distinction, or to all men without distinction. The question which had been discussed with regard to Oxford and

Cambridge, was the admissibility of Dissenters; which in common speech does not mean, I think, Dissenters from Christianity: no one argued, so far as I know, for the admission of avowed unbelievers. I thought that the University of London was intended to solve this question, and I therefore readily joined it.

I do not see the force of the argument about the College in Gower Street; because we admit their students to be examined for degrees, we do not sanction their system any more than we sanction the very opposite system of King's College. Nor does it follow, so far as I see, that University College must have a Professor of Theology, because we expect its members to have a knowledge of the elements of Christianity. University College hopes,—or has not yet ventured to say it does not hope—that its students are provided with this knowledge before they join it.

I am quite clear as to my original position, namely, that if you once get off the purely natural ground of physical science, Philology, and pure Logic—the moment, in short, on which you enter upon any moral subjects—whether Moral Philosophy or History—you must either be Christian or Anti-christian, for you touch upon the ground of Christianity, and you must either take it as your standard of moral judgement, or you must renounce it, and either follow another standard, or have no standard at all. In other words, again, the moment you touch on what alone is education—the forming of the moral principles and habits of man—neutrality is impossible.

The Gower Street College I therefore hold to be Anti-christian, inasmuch as it meddles with moral subjects— having lectures in History—and yet does not require its Professors to be Christians. And so long as the Scriptures were held to contain divine truth on physical science, it was then impossible to give even physical instruction neutrally;—you must either teach it according to God's

principles (it being assumed that God's Word had pro-
nounced concerning it) or in defiance of them. [*SL*,
CLXV, 28 November 1837, pp. 458–9.]

*The last phase. Arnold stands alone and sees little hope for
himself but retirement*

Every single member of the Senate except myself was
convinced of the necessity, according to the Charter, of
giving the Jews Degrees; all were therefore inclined to
make an exemption in their favour as to the New Testament Examination, and thus to make that Examination
not in all cases indispensable. Most were disposed to
make it altogether voluntary, and that was the course
which was at last adopted. [*SL*, CLXXIII, 16 February 1838,
p. 468.]

The Senate were so unanimous in their opinion, that the
admission of unbelievers of all sorts to Degrees in Arts
could not be resisted under the terms of the Charter, that
I should not think it becoming to agitate the question
again. And I think that the voluntary examination which
we have gained is really a great point, and I am strongly
tempted to assist, as far as I can, towards carrying it into
effect. But, on the other hand, the University has solemnly
avowed a principle to which I am totally opposed—
namely, that education need not be connected with
Christianity; and I do not see how I can join in conferring
a degree on those who, in my judgement, cannot be entitled
to it; or in pronouncing that to be a complete education,
which I believe to be no more so than a man without his
soul or spirit is a complete man. Besides, my continuing to
belong to the University, may be ascribed to an unwilling-
ness to offend the Government from interested motives;
all compliances with the powers that be being apt to
be ascribed to unworthy considerations. Again, I feel

exceedingly unwilling to retire on such grounds as mine, while three bishops of our church do not feel it inconsistent with their duty to remain in the University: it seems very like presumption on my part, and a coming forward without authority, when those who have authority, judge that there is no occasion for any protest. My defence must be, that the principle to which I so object, and which appears to me to be involved by a continuance in the University, may not appear to others to be at stake on the present occasion: that I am not professing, therefore, or pretending to be more zealous for Christianity than other members of the Senate, but that what appears to me to be dangerous, appears to them to be perfectly innocent; and that they naturally, therefore, think most of the good which the University will do, while I fear that all that good will be purchased by a greater evil, and cannot, therefore, take any part in the good, as I should wish to do, because, to my apprehension, it will be bought too dearly. [*SL*, CLXXIV, 17 February 1838, pp. 469–70.][21]

VAN DIEMEN'S LAND

The problem of creating a new college in a new land where two religions are involved

What I should like best of all, would be, to see two colleges founded, one an English college, the other a Scotch college, each giving its own Degrees in Divinity, but those Degrees following the Degrees in Arts, which should be given by both as a University. Each College possessing full independence within itself, the education of the members of each would in all respects be according to their respective Churches, while the University authorities, chosen equally from each, would only settle such points as could harmoniously be settled by persons belonging to different Churches.

The decisive objection to this, I suppose, would be the expense. You can have only one college, and I suppose may be thankful even for that. What is next best, then, as it appears to me, is still to provide for the equal, but at the same time the free and sovereign and full-developed action of both Churches within the same college, by the appointment of two clergymen, the one of the English, the other of the Scotch Church, as necessary members of the college always, with the title of Dean, or such other as may be thought expedient, such Deans having the direct charge of the religious instruction generally of their own people; the Dean of that Church to which the Principal for the time being does not belong, being to his own people in all religious matters both Principal and Dean.

It might be possible and desirable to put the office of Principal altogether in commission, and vest it in a Board of which the two Deans should be ex officio members, and three other persons, or one, as it might be thought fit. Local knowledge is required to decide the details. [*SL*, CCLXVII, 16 March 1841, p. 592.]

My own belief is, that our Colleges of Oxford and Cambridge are, with all their faults, the best institutions of the kind in the world,—at least for Englishmen; and therefore I should wish to copy them exactly, if it were possible, for Van Diemen's Land. I only doubted whether it were just to Scotland to give a predominantly English character to the institutions of a *British* colony; but your argument from the establishment of the English law is, I think, a good one, and mixed institutions are to my mind so undesirable, that I would rather have the College Scotch altogether, so far as my own taste is concerned, than that it should represent no Church at all. I have always wished, and I wish it still, that the bases of our own, as of other Churches, should be made wider than they are; but the enlargement, to my mind, should be there, and not in the schools: for it seems a solecism to me that a place of education for the members of a Church should not teach according to that Church, without suppressions of any sort for the sake of accommodating others. [*SL*, CCLXVIII, 4 April 1842, p. 593.][22]

NOTES

1. p. 52   The following extract from one of his sermons gives some indication of his evangelistic style in the pulpit.

2. p. 67   This, in fact, was the solution ultimately arrived at in the 1870 Act.

3. p. 92   Although not strictly written about boys, this inheritance principle was an essential element in Arnold's thinking, and, as the last sentence emphasises, directly impinges on the child.

4. p. 97   In 1831 Arnold took action himself to try to influence the political climate. He published a paper, *Englishman's Register*, and wrote (unsigned) articles for it. This letter refers to his explanations of his actions in the matter.

5. p. 99   In 1836 Arnold wrote an article called 'The Oxford Malignants and Dr Hampden' in the *Edinburgh Review*, but, like all such articles, it was published anonymously. It was a violent denunciation of Newman and Newmanism and aroused bitter controversy. A rumour quickly arose that Arnold himself had written the article, and in this and the next extract Arnold clearly defines his own position *vis à vis* the Trustees. He had already intimated his attitude in *SL*, xxx, 29 July, 1828, p. 80.

6. p. 101   It should be remembered that previously Arnold had been one of the country's main protagonists in church reform from the early days at Rugby to 1836.

7. p. 101   Later, the same year, he writes of his power being 'perfectly absolute' [*SL*, 11, 28 September 1829, p. 218]. See also *SL*, LXXX, 25 June 1834, p. 334.

8. p. 104   This extract is more important than its size. The principle of going far away from Rugby in the holidays was one he kept right to the end. Moreover, he was not usually content to remain at Fox How in the Lake district, but went on extensive journeys on the Continent. This urge to travel was undoubtedly part of his creed concerning the necessity of a teacher to refresh himself continually (the running stream idea).

9. p. 116   The date of this and the following two extracts concerning physical science should be noted. It will be seen that the last extract in time, and the most reasoned in many ways, takes a different view to the others and is far more wistful concerning the advantages of mathematics and science. At one time Arnold had contemplated teaching the next two books of Euclid as well, and may well have done so.

10. p. 117 The teaching of history is also dealt with in *MW*, pp. 246–9.

11. p. 141 This was written in November 1839.

12. p. 147 Dated 17 April 1842, this was written less than two months before Arnold died.

13. p. 147 Wymer N., *Dr Arnold of Rugby*, p. 135. This extract comes from a letter addressed to the Rev. T. T. Penrose, 'To be opened after my death', dated 17 May 1830, i.e. at the beginning of his career at Rugby. The original, with a host of other letters, is to be seen at the Brotherton Library, Leeds University. It is interesting to note that one of his sons, William Delafield, was appointed first Director of Public Instruction in Punjab, and that his portrait is to be seen, to this day, in the Director's office in Lahore—an exciting link which could be the subject of interesting research.

14. p. 149 Amended according to the letter in the Brotherton collection, University of Leeds (Letters to W. A. Greenhill).

15. p. 151 He expressed himself in a similar way about other institutions, including the church and the structure of society.

16. p. 153 This declaration was circulated by Arnold for signature in April/May 1834. See Stanley, pp. 330–1.

17. p. 154 This letter was addressed to Samuel Butler, headmaster of Shrewsbury. This letter deals with the same topic as the previous extract and in some ways is contradictory. The significance here is that the previous extract was a joint declaration and therefore does not completely represent Arnold's personal views. He was in favour of the education of any sect within its own institutions, but there were, of course, complications over citizenship.

18. p. 154 This abuse should be compared with the corresponding one in Public schools which led ultimately to the Clarendon Commission in 1861.

19. p. 156 A note in Stanley (p. 443) states that all these proposals were carried into effect by the Legislature of 1853.

20. p. 161 There is a more elaborate exposition of the practical problems of examining in *SL*, CLVIII, 30 April 1837, pp. 449–52.

21. p. 164 In fact Arnold resigned later the same year, in November; see *SL*, CLXXXVI, 7 November 1838.

22. p. 166 Note that the two references to Van Diemen's Land given here are separated by more than a year.

CHRONOLOGICAL TABLE

Year	Personal, Family, Publications	Educational and Social Events	Military, Political and Foreign
1795	Born 13 June at Cowes, Isle of Wight	Speenhamland system started Rowland Hill born	War with France Series of repressive Acts (1795–1800)
1796			Hoche expedition
1797		Mutinies at Spithead and Nore J. Wilkes dies	Cape St. Vincent and Camperdown
1798	Given Smollett's *History of England* by his father	Income tax Malthus, *Essay on Population*	Napoleon invades Egypt Nile and Vinegar Hill Irish Rebellion
1799			Napoleon first Consul Act banning Reform Societies First Combination Act
1800	Educated till 1803 by Miss Delafield	New Lanark (Robert Owen)	Act of Union Second Combination Act
1801	Father dies	T. W. Hill starts a school First census J. H. Newman born	Addington prime minister Armed Neutrality Aboukir and Copenhagen
1802	Before seven had written blank verse tragedy: *Piercy, Earl of Northumberland*	Mrs Trimmer's *The Guardian* Cobbett, *Register*	Peace of Amiens
1803	School at Warminster	Charlotte Dundas	War with France Invasion scares (till 1805) Hobart Town founded
1804			Pitt prime minister Napoleon emperor
1805		Eldon judgement J. F. D. Maurice born	Trafalgar and Austerlitz
1806	Brother William died	J. Wooll headmaster of Rugby	Pitt dies Ministry of all the Talents Berlin decrees
1807	To Winchester	Slave Trade abolished	Duke of Portland prime minister Treaty of Tilsit

Year	Personal, Family, Publications	Educational and Social Events	Military, Political and Foreign
1808		Lancasterian Association	Wellesley lands in Portugal
1809	At Winchester wrote play *Simon de Montfort* etc. (dates uncertain)	Darwin born Paine dies	Perceval prime minister Corunna and Talavera
1810		Smith's censure of Public Schools Cobbett imprisoned for libel	Torres Vedras
1811	Corpus Christi, Oxford Friends include John Keble and F. T. Coleridge	Midland Luddites (to 1814)	Battles in Spain Prince of Wales, Regent
1812		Mrs Trimmer, *An Essay on Christian Education* Yorkshire Luddites Hampden Club	War with U.S. Wellington enters and leaves Madrid Lord Liverpool prime minister
1813		Comet Owen, *New View of Society*	Wellington enters France
1814	1st class in Litterae Humaniores (aged nineteen)		Toulouse
1815	Fellow of Oriel In Paris Prize Essay: *The Effects of Distant Colonization on the Parent State*	Robert Owen, *Observations* Davy Lamp	Congress of Vienna Corn Law Hundred days Waterloo
1816		Petitition to the House of Commons (Cartwright and Cleary) Cobbett, *Twopenny Register*	
1817	Chancellor's Prize Essay, Latin	R. L. Edgeworth dies	Gagging Acts
1818	Ordained deacon	Letter to Sir Samuel Romilly re charities	Act appointing Charity Commissioners
1819	Settles at Laleham with Buckland	Hill family at Hazelwood	Princess Victoria born Six Acts

Year	Personal, Family, Publications	Educational and Social Events	Military, Political and Foreign
1819		Peterloo Savannah crosses Atlantic	First Factory Act
1820	Brother Matthew dies Marries Mary Penrose	Lant Carpenter, *Principles of Education*	Cato Street Conspiracy George IV Trial of Queen Caroline
1821	1821-7, writing articles on Roman History for the *Encyclopaedia Metropolitana* 1st child, Jane, born	Knox's pamphlet on bill concerning grammar schools	Napoleon dies
1822	2nd child, Matthew, born Visits Whately	*Public Education*	
1823	3rd child, Thomas, born	Quarterly Review article on Early Moral Education	Catholic Association
1824	Visited Lakes and Scotland 2nd daughter born	Combination Act John Cartwright dies	Gaol Acts
1825	Visited Italy Article in Quarterly Review Daughter Mary born	Hazelwood (*Edinburgh Review*) Society for the Diffusion of Useful Knowledge Thoughts of Popular Education (*Edinburgh Review*)	Stockton–Darlington Railway
1826	Son Edward Penrose born Tours Scotland		
1827	Elected headmaster Rugby School (December) Meets Bunsen Tours France and Italy	Keble, *Christian Year* Bruce Castle founded	Canning prime minister Goderich prime minister
1828	Takes up post at Rugby Doctor of Divinity (December)	Trouble at Winchester	Repeal of Test and Corporation Acts Duke of Wellington prime minister

Year	Personal, Family Publications	Educational and Social Events	Military, Political and Foreign
1828	Son William D. born German tour		O'Connell member of Parliament
1829	*Sermons*, vol. 1 *Christian Duty of Granting the Claims of the Roman Catholics* Tours Switzerland and N. Italy	Three-term year at Rugby Clough enters Rugby Metropolitan police	Catholic Emancipation Act
1830	*Thucydides*, vol. 1 Tour in France, Germany, Italy and Switzerland Sees Niebuhr Daughter Susannah born	Birmingham Political Union (Attwood) Classical curriculum attacked (*Edinburgh Review*) Bonamy Price and Prince Lee appointed Rugby Oastler's letter Lyell, *Geology*	French and Belgian revolutions Lord Grey prime minister William IV Liverpool– Manchester Railway
1831	Declines post at Bristol Publishes *Englishman's Register* Writes in *Sheffield Courant* (1831–2) Tours Scotland	Riots in many places National Political Union formed New route for railway at Rugby Cholera epidemic Faraday's experiment Burning of Bristol	Two reform measures defeated
1832	*Sermons*, vol. 2 Daughter born Purchases Fox How Sister Susannah dies Trouble with *Northampton Herald* Cholera near Rugby and school disperses Flogging of March episode	British Magazine starts Hampden gives Bampton lectures Mass meetings at York and elsewhere Shrewsbury School visited by Royalty British Association meeting at Oxford J. Bentham dies	Reform Bill passed
1833	Local and national agitation against Thomas Arnold 6th daughter, Frances, born *Principles of Church Reform*	14 July Keble's Sermon Grand National Union 1st state grant for education First Tract	Railway Act Factory Act

Year	Personal, Family, Publications	Educational and Social Events	Military, Political and Foreign
1833		Emancipation of slaves in empire Wilberforce dies *England and the English*	
1834	Articles in *QJEd* *Sermons*, vol. 3 Arnold warns Pusey Wooll dies Local agitation against Thomas Arnold	Tolpuddle trial New Poor Law Coleridge dies Malthus dies First photograph	Melbourne prime minister Peel prime minister Houses of Parliament burnt
1835	*Thucydides. QJEd* article Fox How completed 5th son, Walter, born Agitation against Thomas Arnold Appointment at London University	Cobbett dies	Melbourne prime minister Municipal Corporations Act
1836	*The Oxford Malignants* Sends two sons to Winchester Agitation against Thomas Arnold Battle with Trustees	S. Butler Bishop of Lichfield London Working Men's Association J. Mill dies *Pickwick*	Nassau balloon
1837	Letters to *Hertford Reformer* (to 1840) Agitation against Thomas Arnold Rugby successes at Oxford and Cambridge G. Cotton appointed In France	Labour troubles Birmingham Political Union revived Registration of births, marriages and deaths Constable dies	William IV dies Queen Victoria
1838	Bunsen at Rugby Resigns Fellowship at London	Froude, *Remains* Bishop of Oxford objects to the *Tracts* Chartist 'National Education' Resistance to Poor Law Railway and gasometer at Rugby Sirius crosses Atlantic	Electric Telegraph

Year	Personal, Family, Publications	Educational and Social Events	Military, Political and Foreign
1839	Two Sermons on the Interpretation of Prophesy *On the Division and Mutual relations of Knowledge* Continental journey Plans Society (to 1842) Wratislaw case against Rugby School— Langdale's judgement Trouble in the school	First Chartist Convention The People's Charter Newport Rising Penny Postage *Voyage of the Beagle* British Association in Birmingham	Anti-Corn-Law League
1840	Travel in Italy Offer of Manchester College Successes of Old Rugbeians at Oxford	Chartist troubles	Queen Victoria marries Opium War New Zealand annexed
1841	*Sermons*, vol. 4 Travel on continent Professor of Modern History (Oxford) Health problems at Rugby School	Tract 90 Lovell's 'Chartism'	Peel prime minister O'Connell agitates
1842	Meets Newman (2 February) Carlyle at Rugby Illness and recovery (May) Death, Sunday, 12 June	Chartist Convention Income tax	

SELECT BIBLIOGRAPHY

WORKS BY DR ARNOLD

The Christian Duty of Granting the Claims of the Roman Catholics (with a postscript), 1829.

'The Effects of Distant Colonization on the Parent State'. A prize essay, 1815.

Encyclopaedia Metropolitana. Articles on Roman History, 1821–7 (republished as *History of the later Roman Commonwealth,* 1845).

The Englishman's Register, 1831—articles signed 'A'.

Fragment on the Church, 1844.

Hertford Reformer, 1837–41. Letters to the Editor.

History of Rome. vol. 1, 1838.

History of Rome. vol. 2, 1840.

History of Rome. vol. 3, 1842 (unfinished).

Introductory Lectures on Modern History, 1842.

The Miscellaneous Works of Thomas Arnold, 1845.

*'On the Discipline of Public Schools'. *QJEd*, vol. IX, No. XVIII, 1835.

On the Divisions and Mutual Relations of Knowledge. A lecture, 1839.

'The Oxford Malignants and Dr Hampden'. *Edinburgh Review,* April 1836.

Principles of Church Reform, and a postscript, 1833.

Psalms and Hymns. Selected for the Use of Rugby Chapel, 1835.

*'Rugby School'. *QJEd*, vol. VII, No. XIV, 1834.

Sermons, 1829 (vol. 1 of 1878 edition, *Christian Life*).

Sermons, 1832 (vol. 2 of 1878 edition, *Christian Life at School*).

Sermons, 1834 (vol. 3 of 1878 edition, *Christian Life and Doctrine*).

Sermons, Christian Life, its Course, its Hindrances, and its Helps, 1841 (vol. 4 of 1878 edition).

Sermons, Christian Life, its Hopes, its Fears and its Close, 1842 (vol. 5 of 1878 edition).

Sermons, Chiefly on the Interpretation of Scripture, 1845. (vol. 6 of 1878 edition).

The Sheffield Courant, 1832. Thirteen letters on our social condition addressed to the Editor.

Thucydides. vol. 1, 1830.

176 SELECT BIBLIOGRAPHY

Thucydides. vol. 2, 1833.
Thucydides. vol. 3, 1835.
Two Sermons on the Interpretation of Prophecy, Preached in the Chapel of Rugby School (with notes), 1839.

* These are included, with other extracts, in *The Miscellaneous Works of Thomas Arnold*.

Arnold was also an energetic letter writer. The main source is in Stanley, A. P. *Life and Correspondence of Dr. Arnold*. 2 vols, 1844 (see p. viii). Other letters are in the British Museum, British Transport Commission Archives, Brotherton Library (University of Leeds), Dr Williams Library, Lord Denbigh's collection, and in the books by Whitridge and Wymer listed below.

BIOGRAPHIES AND STUDIES

Bamford, T. W. *Thomas Arnold*, 1960.
Campbell, R. J. *Thomas Arnold*, 1927.
Findlay, J. J. *Arnold of Rugby, His School Life and Contributions to Education*, 1897.
Fitch, J. G. *Thomas and Matthew Arnold and Their Influence on English Education*, 1897.
Sanders, C. R. *Coleridge and the Broad Church Movement*. 1942.
Selfe, R. E. *Dr Arnold of Rugby*, 1889.
Stanley, A. P. *Life and Correspondence of Dr Arnold*, 2 vols. 1844. (Reprinted many times. A teachers' edition with a preface by Sir Joshua Fitch was published in 1901. A section towards the end of this work is a travelling journal.)
Strachey, L. *Eminent Victorians*, 1918.
Tuckwell, W. *Pre-Tractarian Oxford*, 1909.
Whitridge, A. *Dr Arnold of Rugby*, 1928 (includes a study by Sir Michael Sadler).
Willey, B. *Nineteenth Century Studies*, 1955.
Williamson, E. L. *The Liberalism of Thomas Arnold*, 1964.
Woodward, F. J. *The Doctor's Disciples*, 1954.
Wymer, N. *Dr Arnold of Rugby*, 1953.

INDEX

American revolution, 2, 33
aristocracy, 17–18
Aristotle, 3, 12, 16, 35, 101, 107, 114, 119
armed forces, 19, 25, 144–6; see also professions
Arnold, Mary, 37
Arnold, Matthew, 28, 34, 36
Arnold, Thomas: character, 2–5, 8, 23–5; education of sons, 19–20; educational views, 19–29; examiner, 157; headmastership, 27–8; idea of his life, 156; influence of family, 29, 34; influence on education, 35–7; letters, viii, 37–40; life, 169–74, and problems, 1–5; paradoxical features, 4–5, 23; religious ideas and education, 5–12, 31–2; salary, 25; social ideas and education, 12–19, 33–4; sources of ideas, 29–36; staff, 8, 25–7; works, 175–6; writing, 37–40
Attwood, T., 34

Bacon, F., 61, 112
Bentham, J., 34
Bible, 68, 83
boarding, 20, 128–9, 134
book instruction, 60–1, 65
Boswell, J., 61
Bowdler, J., 31, 48
Bowdler, T., 32
boyhood, 20–1, 25, 31; customs, 50; effect of boys on boys, 84–6, 138–9; evil, 50–3, 83–93; need to shorten, 20, 31, 79–83; problems, 78–93; see also, childhood, evil, evils
boys: age and cruelty, 131; evils aggravated, 135; fears, 136–7; masters as enemies, 51, 89–90; pollution of new boys, 52–3; shame, 137; sins weighed, 91–2; society, 135–9; see also fagging, public schools, punishment, Rugby schoolboys, schools, Sixth Form
Broad Church Movement, 30, 32
bullying, 9, 86–9
Bulwer, L., 35
Busby, R., 36
Butler, J., 30, 61
Butler, S., 32

Cambridge university, 28–9, 115, 118; Dissenters, 152–3, 157–8; see also colleges
careers, 144–50
Cartwright, J., 34
Catechism, 68–70
Chartist, 18
childhood, boyhood and manhood, 10, 20–1, 79–83
childhood to manhood transition: aspects of, 79–83; death and salvation, 83; need to hasten, 79–83
childishness, 9, 141
Christian education, 49, 68–77; boys and, 72, 134–5; examinations, 160–1; national, 156–8; schools, 68, 134–5; unitarians, 76–7, 160; see also citizenship, education, religious education, religious instruction
christian standards, 11–12
christianity: role in future state, 17; humanity and, 159; nationhood and, 156–8

church and state, 6–7, 156–8
citizenship and: business, 56;
   christianity, 15, 17, 156–8;
   property, 15–16; race, 15;
   religion, 6–7, 15, 17
Clarkson, T., 33
classical education, 106–14;
   justification, 106–8, 113–14;
   methods, 108–13; modern
   relevance, 108–9; transfer of
   training, 108; translation,
   108–13
classics, 2, 21–2; enlivening,
   114; teaching of 21–2, 34,
   41, 106–14; see also Greek,
   Latin, translation
clergy: parish and school, 103;
   recruitment, 150; as schoolmasters, 94–6, 99; status,
   94, 150
Cobbett, W., 34
Coleridge, S. T., 30–1, 61
colleges at universities:
   Dissenters, 157; powers,
   153–6; standards, 152
colonies, 13, 147
commercial schools, 54, 57, 94, 96
Communion, 94
companionship, evil aspects,
   86–7, 90–1
construing, 108–10, 112, 115
corporal punishment, 31,
   121–2; age of boys, 123–4,
   126–7; see also bullying,
   discipline, flogging,
   punishment
cruelty, see bullying
curriculum, 21–3

Darwin, C., 10
Davison, J., 30
Dickens, C., 32
discipline, 34–5, 41, 125–6;
   parents, 97; see also bullying
   corporal punishment,
   expulsion, fagging, flogging,
   independence

disobedience, 9, 86–7, 89
dispensaries, 64–7
Dissenters, 77, 152–4, 157–8,
   161; pamphlet, 157
drunkenness, 9, 86–8, 138

Edinburgh Review, 29, 38, 99
education: centralisation fear,
   67; christianity and, 7–8,
   31–2, 73–4, 153, 157–8, 163;
   consequences, 55–6; dynamic
   process, 102; elective
   franchise, 55; emigration,
   14, 65, 148–9; independence,
   67; leaving age, 58–9; lower-
   class, 36, 58–67; management,
   66–7; middle-class, 35–6,
   54–8; national-christian, 67,
   156–8; political power, 55;
   property, 16, 64–5; purpose,
   102, 114; social classes,
   45–67
Edward VI, 30, 156
emigration, 13–14, 65, 148–9
empire, 19, 146–8; and the
   middle class, 14, 147–8;
   see also emigration, India
English: composition, 54,
   118–19; foreign words,
   111–12; grammar, 54;
   style, 112
English schools, 59, 94, 96
Establishment, 157–8
Eton, 26, 28, 32–3, 35, 36
evil: aggravated, 135;
   Arnold and, 8–11, 31; bond
   of, 86–7, 90–1; and childhood, boyhood, 78, 137–9;
   and citizenship, 92–3;
   concept of, 9–12;
   doubts on origin, 74–6;
   inheritance, of, 92–3; and
   innocence, 78; of literature,
   141–3; and teachers, 78
evils, six at school, 9, 86
examinations, 23–4, 117–21;
   dangers of, 118; increasing

stress of, 117–18; at London university, 160–3; written papers inadequate for, 120; *see also* viva voce

exhaustion, mental, 80–2

expulsion, 10–11, 31, 105, 126–7

extravagance, 9, 137–8

faculties, 114, 118, 120; *see also* transfer of training

fagging, 18, 121, 128–36; abuses, 130–2; benefits, 130, 133–4; in boarding schools, 128–9, 134–5; as device of government, 128–33; legality, of 133; physical strength, 130–2; servility, 133–4; staff shortage and, 128–9, 132

falsehood, 9, 86, 88

fear, 122–3

Fielden, J., 34

fines at Oxford, 154–5

flogging, 11, 121–7; *see also* bullying, punishment

Forster, W. E., 36

foundations, 36, 67, 95

freedom and property, 13–14

French revolution, 2, 32–3, 98

Gabell, H. D., 34, 36, 110

gentry, 17–18

girls, education: examinations, 120–1; lack of degree, 120

Goethe, J. W., 114

Governing part of the school, fagging, 129–33; nature of, 128–9; responsibility of, 129–30; *see also* fagging, sixth form

Gower Street college, 161–2; *see also* London university

great men and education, 60–1

Greece, 106–8, 112, 117

Greek, 38, 54, 106, 108–9, 111

Hampden, R. D., 30

Harrow, 22, 26, 32

Hawkins, E., 30, 32

headmasters: anonymity, 99–100; elite, 33; governing bodies, 28, 97–100; politics, 97–100; public school cult, 32–3; religion, 99; rights and duties, 27–8, 97–100; role, 36; scandals, 99–100

history, 54, 113–14, 117, 141, 159, 162

home influence, 47–8, 52; *see also* parental influence, public schools

Homer, 106, 111, 114

Hooker, R., 30, 112

housing, lower-class, 14, 66; *see also* town-planning

Hughes, T., 34

Hull, W. W., 31

idleness, 9, 11, 86–7, 89–90, 136–41, 145

independence and punishment, 121–2

India, 14, 19, 147–8; *see also* empire,

inferiority feeling, 121–2, 125

information, useful and useless, 113–14

Ingles, H., 34

innocence, 11, 78; *see also* evil, sin

instruction and education, 59, 68

Islam, 7

Jacobinism, 122, 133

Jews, 7, 15, 77, 161, 163

Johnson, S., 61, 112

Jung, C., 10

Knox, V., 32

Lake poets, 29; *see also* Coleridge, Wordsworth

Latin, 38, 54, 106, 108–12
law and lawyers, 19, 24–5, 149
leadership, 18–19, 35, 146–7
letters, 37–40
liberal education, 55–6
libraries, 66–7
logic, 159, 162
London university, 7, 29,
  118, 120, 156–64; *see also*
  Gower Street college,
Longley, C. T., 32
lower class, 14–18; christian
  education of, 68–72; and
  emigration, 147–9; responsibility for, 66–7

Malthus, T. R., 12, 16, 34
man, two businesses of, 55–8
management and lower-class
  education, 66–7
manliness, 11–12, 35, 82–4, 130;
  christian, 11–12, 83
masters, *see* teachers
mathematics, 22, 116
mechanics' Institutes, 60, 62;
  weakness of, 62–3
medicine and medical students,
  19, 24, 149–50; low morals,
  117, 149–50
middle-class schools, 94–7:
  curriculum, 54; reading
  attainment, 54; and Local
  Universities, 96–7;
Moberly, G., 32
money: debts, 137; stealing, 53
moral education, 59, 62, 159
moral philosophy, 159, 162
morality and boys, 91
More, H., 31
Moslems, 7, 161

Newman, J. H., and Newmanism, 5, 6, 27, 30, 32, 38;
  see also Oxford Movement,
  Tractarians
newspapers and education, 57,
  59

Nicene Creed, 70
Noetics, 29–30

Oastler, R., 34
Owen, R., 16, 34
Oxford Malignants, 99
Oxford Movement, 3, 5–6;
  see also Newman
Oxford University, 1, 13, 28–9,
  114–15, 118–19, 151–8;
  dissenters, 152–3, 157–8;
  entrance examination, 152;
  reform, 151–6; residence,
  153–6; science, 116–17;
  standards, 152; *see also*
  colleges

pain, 122–3
Parental influence, 20, 97,
  136–8; *see also* home influence
parks and recreation, *see*
  town-planning
parochial schools, 94
Paul, St, 87, 103
philology, 114–15, 162
physical science, 62, 115–16,
  162; compared with
  philosophy 116; at university,
  116–17
Physical state and education, 63
Place, F., 34
Plato, 3, 35, 101, 107, 116
poetry, 141, 159
political education, 59
political power, 57
poor, The, 12–16; education
  of, 58–9, 63–7, 148–9; rich
  and, 72–3, 150; school-
  leaving age of, 58–9
popular literature, 9, 141–3
population: crisis, 12, 13;
  and property, 16–17;
  theory, 12–18
prefects, *see* leadership, public
  schools, sixth form
Price, B., 26
Principles of Church Reform, 6

private education, 35, 48; necessary for some, 127

professional education, 55; and examinations, 117; liberal education, 55–6

professions, 5, 24–5, 149–50; army, navy, 144–6; status, 36;

profligacy, 9, 86–8

property, 13–14, 16–17; as education, 64–5

public schools: Arnold's views, 19–20, 35, 45–53; benefits, 20, 35; Bowdler, 48–9; cooperation, 105; education, 45–53; Empire, 146–7; England and Scotland, 128; historical significance, 45–6; home effects, 46–8; leadership 35, 48, 146–7; nurseries of vice, 48–51; role, 14, 35; size, 46, 134; traditions, 45–6, 50–1

punishment, 122–7; and morals, 125, 127; see also discipline

reading, 54; not education, 58–9

reform, 2–4, 148; age and, 100–1; church, 6–7, 100; church and state, 156; love and, 151; national survey, 3; public schools, 5

Reform Bill, 17, 18, 55, 98

Reformers, The Edward VI, 30, 156, 158

religious attitude, 74; education, 62, 64, 69; instruction, 54, 69–71; societies and poor, 64

Roman Catholics, 5–6, 160–1

Rome, 106–8, 112, 117

Rousseau, J.-J., 32

Rugby school, 18, 20, 22, 24–6, 32, 41, 52, 99, 101, 104, 113, 143; curriculum, 22–3, 35, 106–14

Rugby schoolboys; codes, 87; duties of four ages, 83–6; power, 84–6

sceptical doubts, 74–6

schools: leaving age, 58–9; regulations, 137; richer classes, 94–5; self-governing, 35, 101; six evils, 86–91;

secondary education, 96

Sermons, viii, 38–9

sex, 9–10

Shakespeare, 61, 106, 111, 114

sin: Arnold and, 9–12; original, 9–11, 31; see also evil

Sixth form, 104, 114, 135

Slaney, R. A., 34

slavery, 13–14

social: evils and church, 64; ideas and education, 12–19; mobility and property, 65; radicalism, 33–4

sports, 132

staff, public school, 8, 25–7; as dons, 26, 36; meetings, 36; primness of, 10; role of, 26; and sex, 10

Stanley, A. P., viii

teachers: clergy, 26, 94–6; diversions and, 104; expelling, 105; intellectual and moral, 95–6; licence, 95; liveliness, 103–4; middle-class, 28, 35–6, 95–7; status, 8, 26–7, 32, 94–7; student attitude, 102; study and, 103; sympathy, 103

Temple, F., 34, 36

town-planning, 66

Tractarians, 5–6; see also Newman, Oxford Movement

transfer of training, 21; see also faculties

translation, 109–113; extempore, 118–19; *see also*
construing
Trimmer, Mrs, 32
Trustees, 28, 95, 99

Unitarians, 7–8, 15, 76–7, 152,
160; and christian education,
76–7, 160; and university,
153–4
universities: admissions, 15,
152, 157–8, 161; local, 28,
36, 96; power of colleges,
153–6; Scottish, 29; *see also*
Cambridge, colleges, London,
Oxford

Van Dieman's Land, 100, 140,
164–6
vice and public schools, 49–50;
see also evil

viva voce examiations,
118–20; at university, 112, 115
vocational education, 24–5, 54

Wakefield, E. G., 34
Whately, R., 30–1.
Wilberforce, W., 31, 33
Winchester, 20, 26, 110, 121,
152, 155; fagging at, 130–3
wisdom: and youth, 79; and
knowledge, 81
Wooll, J., 20
Wordsworth, W., 33–4
work at school: agreeable and
disagreeable, 139–40;
incentives, 139
writers, ancient and modern,
106–7, 111–12

youth, analysis of, 82–3;
see also boyhood, boys

For EU product safety concerns, contact us at Calle de José Abascal, 56–1°, 28003 Madrid, Spain or eugpsr@cambridge.org.